A TASTE OF ROME

A TASTE OF ROME

TRADITIONAL FOOD
BY THEODORA FITZGIBBON

Period photographs specially prepared by
GEORGE MORRISON

1975 · HOUGHTON MIFFLIN COMPANY BOSTON

Library of Congress Cataloging in Publication Data
FitzGibbon, Theodora.
A taste of Rome.
1. Cookery, Italian.   I. Morrison, George, fl.
1968-   II. Title.
TX723.F57   1975   641.5′945   75-6539
ISBN 0-395-20448-8

Printed in the United States of America

W 10 9 8 7 6 5 4 3 2 1

For Speer Ogle, Henry McConnachie and Vernon Jarratt
with affection and many thanks for all their
kindness and assistance.

ACKNOWLEDGMENTS

We both want to thank several very good friends who gave us so much kind assistance during the preparation of this book. Particularly, Mr Speer Ogle, Mr Henry McConnachie and Mr Vernon Jarratt whose help in so many ways was invaluable. Also Desmond and Florence O'Grady for making our stay in Rome a real 'taste' of the city.

We also convey our thanks to the Contessa Bedini of Babington's Tea Rooms, Signora Grimaldi and her son, Signor Grimaldi, of the Caffè Greco, Signor Angelo Bettoja of the Massimo d'Azeglio restaurant, Signor Mazzarella of Piperno's restaurant, also the director of Passetto's restaurant for valuable photographs, recipes, and other information. The directors of the Grand Hotel and G. Ranieri also gave us valuable time and help, and Signor Barberi lent us one of the fine photographs from his caffè in the Via del Teatro Marcello.

We particularly want to thank the Irish Embassy in Rome who went to great trouble on our behalf, and without whose help the book would not have been as complete. Also the Italian Cultural Institute in Dublin, who lent us books and were generally helpful. Once again I have to thank, very much, Roisin Kirwan of my local library for finding all the out-of-print books, without which I could not have written this book.

Professore Oreste Ferrari and his assistant Signorina Miralia of the Gabinetto Fotografico Nazionale not only supplied us with many photographs but were most kind and courteous during our researches. Likewise Dr Mario Praz and his assistant at the Fondazione Primoli.

Photographs on pages 8 (G.664), 13 (N.2059), 15 (E.59940), 16 (N.1589), 20, 23 (N.5097), 24, 27 (N.982), 38 (E.69022), 40, 46 (C.940), 53 (N.1561), 57 (N.613), 60 (N.5943), 65, 69, 73, 77, 80, 82 (C.1143), 99 (N.2180), 100, 103 (N.1950), 104 (D.3338), 106 (G.694), 116 (E.69028), 118 (N.1583) by kind permission of the Gabinetto Fotografico Nazionale.

Photographs on pages 7, 18, 29, 37, 62, 70, 87, 91, 108, 112 by kind permission of the Fondazione Primoli.

Photographs on pages 4, 31, 42, 55, 58, 111, 114 by kind permission of Signora Grimaldi of the Caffè Greco.

Photographs on pages 79, 92 by kind permission of Signor Angelo Bettoja.

Photographs on pages 2, 49 by knid permission of Contessa Bedini.

Photographs on pages xii, 44, 67, 89, 97 by kind permission of Dr Thomas and Mr Ward, of the Science Museum, London.

Photograph on page 10 was kindly given by Passetto's restaurant: on page 34 by courtesy of Signor Mazzarella of Piperno's restaurant: on page 75 by courtesy of Signor Ernesto Barberi, of the Caffè del Teatro Marcello: on page 50 by courtesy of Raccolta Incisa della Rocchetta – Rocchetta Tanare: on page 95 by courtesy of Raccolta Becchetti, Rome.

The photograph on page 32 is by courtesy of the Museo di Roma.

Endpaper photographs by George Morrison from details of a drawing by F. Ferrari, 1837, belonging to Mr Henry McConnachie.

CONTENTS

'. . . tens of thousands line the Corso on both sides, when the horses are brought out into the Piazza – to the foot of that same column which, for centuries, looked down upon the games and chariot-races in the Circus Maximus.

'At a given signal, they are started off. Down the live lane, the whole length of the Corso, they fly like the wind: riderless, as all the world knows: with shining ornaments upon their backs, and twisted in their plaited manes: and with heavy little balls stuck full of spikes, dangling at their sides, to goad them on. The jingling of these trappings, and the rattling of their hoofs upon the hard stones; the dash and fury of their speed along the echoing street; nay, the very cannon that are fired – these noises are nothing to the roaring of the multitude: their shouts: the clapping of their hands. But it is soon over – almost instantaneously. More cannon shake the town. The horses have plunged into the carpets put across the street to stop them; the goal is reached; the prizes are won (they are given, in part, by the poor Jews, as a compromise for not running foot-races themselves); and there is an end to that day's sport.'

A description of the Corso horse-race (see endpapers) from *Pictures from Italy*, CHARLES DICKENS, 1845.

I INTRODUCTION

'The tourists tell you all about these things, and I am afraid of stumbling on their language when I enumerate what is so well known.' Thus wrote Percy Bysshe Shelley in 1821 and I cannot but feel a similar trepidation when writing an introduction to a book about Rome.

From our earliest years we have known perhaps more about Rome than our native village or city, whether by learning Roman history at school, from a gaudily coloured print of St Peter's church, or a water-colour of the Colosseum painted by a long-dead relative upon the walls of a bedroom in our childhood. The eighteenth-century writer Johann Winckelmann said: 'Rome is the high school which is open to all the world', and this is just as true today as when it was written.

We all owe an enormous amount to the culture which the Roman legions brought to Europe: it is part of our heritage which embraces even many of the foods we eat. Lucullus brought back cherries from Asia after his campaigns, and it is thought that the many wild cherry trees which line the old Roman roads in England come from the stones dropped by the soldiers who were eating cherries while on the march. The system of cultivating oysters in beds was invented in the fifth century B.C. by Sergius Orata. Improvements in growing wheat, and grapes, all stem from Roman days in Britain, not forgetting the opening up of many lead mines. A speciality in the West country of England is eating snails, where they are known as 'wall-fish'. Under the shadow of the Mendip Hills, where the Romans first introduced edible snails into Britain, Mr Paul Leyton of the Miner's Arms not only serves snails regularly on the menu, but also employs a snail-catcher.

Our word 'sauce' comes from the Latin *salsus*, which means salted, and the Romans might almost be said to have invented sauces, for in general they disliked foods that were not heavily spiced and dished up elaborately. Almost every savoury dish contained *garum* or *liquamen*, a sauce made from small fish soaked in brine, which must have resembled the old-fashioned Harvey's sauce, or today is similar to Worcestershire. *Garum* was used instead of salt for flavouring and from the earliest days factories were set up for making it. In the ruins of Pompeii a jar was found with 'Best strained liquamen. From the factory of Umbricus Agathopus' written on the side of it. *Defrutum* and *passum* were sweet sauces made from pressed grapes, the juices reduced by boiling. Many sauces were thickened by wheat starch (like our cornflour), called *amulum*.

Much has been written about Roman feasts with the larks' tongues and dormice in honey. They are satirized in Trimalchio's feast in the *Satyricon* of Petronius. The grand Roman dinner consisted of three courses: the *gustatio* or *gustum*, which might be of eggs served in different ways, raw or cooked vegetables such as asparagus, cucumber, mushrooms or lettuce; oysters and other shellfish; snails or dormice in a sweet sauce. With this course *mulsum* was served, a drink made from honey steeped for a month in grape must, or better still according to Pliny, dry white wine. According to Pliny it had medicinal qualities as well. (The proportions given by Columella are roughly about 5 oz. honey to a pint of wine, and it was strained before use.)

The *Primae mensae* was the main course, containing meats and poultry in various forms and eaten with a rough wine or wine and water. The last course, or *Secundae mensae*, originally also served savoury dishes, but later on it became the sweet course as we know it today. It was with this course, and after the meal, that serious drinking began. Almonds were often eaten with this course, for the Romans thought that they kept them sober. This could account for the serving of salted almonds with drink today.

The origin of *Pasta* is hard to trace: some say that is was brought from China by Marco Polo, others that it was brought by the Ostrogoths from the East, after their invasion of Italy in A.D. 405. Whatever its origin it was an immediate success. However, it was not married with the tomato until the Middle Ages, when a monk called Serenio brought back some tomato seeds from China. It was to be very much later that it arrived as a regular item on our menus, in these islands.

In the sixteenth century Catherine de' Medici brought her chefs to France when she married the Dauphin (who afterwards became Henry II) and it was one of her cooks, Buontalenti, who introduced ices to the French court. Many vegetables now commonplace, such as small green peas (*petit pois*) (see pages 1 and 109), broccoli, Savoy cabbages, artichokes and haricot beans, together with their methods for cultivation and cooking, were introduced to France early in the seventeenth century by Marie de' Medici.

Augustus Hare, in the introduction to his excellent book *Walks in Rome*, stresses that for those who wish to take away more than a mere surface impression of Rome, '. . . it is, never to see too much; never to try to "do" Rome'. In this book, which is simply a taste of Rome, I too would urge you to savour slowly all the magnificent ingredients that go to make up that wonderful and everlasting city. In Samuel Roger's words, written in 1820: 'The memory in Rome sees more than the eye.'

THEODORA FITZGIBBON,

Atlanta,   Atlanta,
Deilginis,   Dalkey,
Baile Atha Cliath.   Dublin.

PISELLI ALLA ROMANA

'. . . Paul of Tarsus, who passed into Rome under the Arch of Drusus, upon whom the shadow of the tomb of Caius Cestius fell as he passed out of Rome to his martyrdom . . .'

Augustus Hare, *Walks in Rome*, 1871

'The Arch of Drusus was decreed by the senate in honour of the second son of the empress Livia, by her first husband, Tiberius Nero. On its summit are the remains of the aqueduct by which Caracalla carried water to his baths. The arch once supported an equestrian statue of Drusus, two trophies, and a seated female figure representing Germany.' Ibid. (Drusus was the father of the Emperor Claudius and died during a campaign on the Rhine in 9 B.C., his body being brought back by his stepfather, Augustus.)

Nearby is the Porta San Sebastiano, which has two semicircular towers of the Aurelian Wall, on a base of marble blocks, thought to be plundered from the tombs on the Via Appia. 'It was here that the senate and people of Rome received in state the last triumphant procession which has entered the city by the Via Appia, that of Marc Antonio Colonna, after the victory of Lepanto in 1571. As in the processions of the old Roman generals, the children of the conquered prince were forced to adorn the triumph of the victor who rode into Rome attended by all the Roman nobles, "in abito di grande formalita", preceded by the standard of the fleet.' Ibid.

PISELLI ALLA ROMANA
(Peas cooked the Roman way)

The green peas which grow near Rome are very small, sweet and tender. To make this dish properly only small, young peas must be used, before they become floury.

2 lb (1 kg.) peas before shelling	3 slices of lean sliced ham, preferably raw, but cooked will do
1 small onion, peeled and sliced very thinly	3 tablespoons water
3 heaped tablespoons butter	salt
a pinch of sugar	freshly ground pepper

Heat the butter until foaming but not brown, then lightly soften the onion, but on no account let it brown. Add the shelled peas, sugar and water and cook for 5 minutes. Then add the ham cut into very thin strips, salt and pepper. Cover and cook gently for a further 5–7 minutes, when the peas should be cooked. Increase cooking time slightly if they are still too firm. Serve at once.

Enough for 4.

This also makes a fresh, delicate accompaniment to boiled rice or pasta.

The Arch of Drusus, near the Porta Appia, c. 1841.

SCANDIAN PANCAKE ROLLS

In 1818 there were two thousand English people living in Rome, one-seventeenth of the population, which prompted the poet Byron to say that Rome was 'pestilent with them'. Many of the descendants of this large colony were in Rome at the end of the last century and the young ladies of artistic inclination studied painting and other arts. Miss Cargill, together with her friend Miss Anna Maria Babington, started Babington's Tea Rooms in 1893 (see page 48).

SCANDIAN PANCAKE ROLLS
(Chicken and mushroom stuffed pancakes)

A regular item on Babington's menu today. Recipe kindly given by Contessa Bedini.

FOR THE PANCAKES
4 eggs
½ pint (1 cup) (0·285 l.) milk
9 oz. (2 scant cups) (250 g.) flour
pinch of baking powder
1 tablespoon sugar
2 tablespoons melted margarine
pinch of salt

1 small chicken about 2¼ lb. (1 kg.) cooked in
6 tablespoons olive oil with 1 teaspoon salt
½ lb. (227 g.) mushrooms lightly cooked in
6 tablespoons oil with 1 teaspoon salt
¼ pint (½ cup) (0·142 l.) white wine
½ pint (1 cup) (0·285 l.) stock
2 tablespoons flour

Cook the chicken with the oil and salt for about ¾ hour and leave to get cold enough to skin and take from the bone. Then chop it up finely. To the pan juices add the white wine and boil up, reducing to about half. Reserve this stock. Cook the mushrooms in oil and salt and chop them finely and combine with the chicken.

Meanwhile make the pancakes by beating the eggs with the sugar, salt and flour then add the milk and beat well with a rotary beater. When well mixed add the baking powder and the melted margarine. In a pan 8 inches across, heat a knob of margarine and make a pancake to fit the pan (about 2 tablespoons batter), turn when one side is golden and do the other. Repeat until the mixture is finished (12 pancakes) and drain on absorbent paper.

Mix 2 tablespoons flour into the chicken stock, heat up, stirring all the time, then add ½ pint (1 cup) (0·285 l.) stock (a bouillon cube dissolved will do), stir well until the mixture is thick and creamy and add the chicken and mushrooms. Fill each pancake with 2 tablespoons of the chicken and mushroom mixture, roll up and lay side by side in a fireproof dish.

FOR THE CHEESE SAUCE
12 formaggini Bel Paese (approx. 1 oz. each) or similar processed cheese
1 tablespoon butter or margarine
4 tablespoons water

Heat the sauce ingredients over a low heat until it resembles a bechamel sauce. Spoon this over the pancakes and heat up in a moderate oven (350°F.) for about 20 minutes. Serves 6.

Interior of Count da Pozzo's 'Fine Arts Academy for Young Ladies', Via S. Nicola da Tolentino, April 1900. Count da Pozzo subsequently married Miss Cargill (on his left in photograph) and their daughter, Contessa Bedini, now runs Babington's Tea Rooms.

POLLO NOVELLO ALLA MASSIMILIANO

The Via Condotti is so called from the conduits built by Pope Gregory XIII (1572–85) to bring the waters of the Acqua Vergine (see page 56) to this part of the town. It is a famous street for shoppers, for it contains beautiful shops full of hand-embroidered linens, ties, jewellery and other luxury items. It leads off the Piazza di Spagna at one end and into the Piazza Borghese with its magnificent Palazzo Borghese, begun in 1590 by Martino Longhi the Elder. There is a small market in the piazza selling books and pictures. In the Via Mario dei Fiori (the first turning past the Caffè Greco) is the historic restaurant Ranieri, which was founded in 1843 by a Frenchman called Renault. It became well known for its good food and during the French occupation was patronized by high-ranking French officers and foreign residents. Its real historical interest begins, however, in 1865 when it was bought by Giuseppe Ranieri, who had been chef to Queen Victoria and then to the ill fated Emperor Maximilian, whom he accompanied to Mexico. After the Emperor's arrest the Empress Carlotta, who had lost her reason, brought Ranieri back to Rome where she tried in vain to get Papal support. Ranieri stayed in Rome and took over the restaurant, which is continued in the old style today by his direct descendant, with its damask-covered walls and superb food. Many distinguished people have left their signatures in the visitors' book and the restaurant is mentioned in the books of Gide, Anatole France, Stendhal, Paul Bourget and Destree. For information about the Caffè Greco see pages 30, 43, 54.

POLLO NOVELLO ALLA MASSIMILIANO
(Young Chicken Maximilian, named in honour of the Emperor)

1 young chicken about 2 lb. (1 kg.)	salt
	freshly ground pepper
1 crushed bay leaf	1 jigger of brandy
3 tablespoons olive oil	

Split the chicken in two, by running a sharp knife along the back, then brush it well with oil, rubbing it into both sides. Then season it and rub in the crumbled bay leaf. Heat up the grill and first grill the inside for about 15 minutes, then turn over and do the other side, making sure that the oil and seasonings are not rubbed off. Cook for the same length of time, or until it is evenly golden brown. Put on to a hot serving dish, and keep warm, meanwhile warming up the ladle of brandy. Pour over the chicken at table, and set alight, shaking the dish slightly until the flames subside.

Serves 2.

Ranieri's is also well known for its crêpes, egg dishes and desserts; see page 74.

The Caffè Greco, Via Condotti, c. 1900.

BISTECCA ALLA FIORENTINA

It seems virtually true that 'All roads lead to Rome' when one thinks of Buffalo Bill's Circus and Annie Oakley being in Rome in 1890. Annie Oakley's real name was Phoebe Anne Oakley Mozee. She was born in 1860, lived until 1926, and was famous as a sharpshooter. She was also a magnificent horsewoman and in her late twenties joined Colonel Cody's (Buffalo Bill) circus and travelled not only around the United States, but also to many European capitals. One feels that to enable her to perform such hazards, daily, steak must have figured largely in her diet.

BISTECCA ALLA FIORENTINA
(Steak Florentine)

Although this enormous rib steak is a speciality of Tuscany, many Roman restaurants serve it, particularly Tuscan restaurants such as La Fontanella in the Largo di Fontanella Borghese. It is so large and so succulent that there is never room for anything else on the plate, but a side portion of Bean Salad is good with it.

1 large T-bone steak	freshly ground black pepper
2 tablespoons olive oil	salt
1 crushed garlic clove	a knob of butter
1 teaspoon lemon juice	

Rub the steak with the oil, garlic, lemon juice and pepper on both sides and leave for about an hour. This steak is best cooked over charcoal, but if this is not available, then preheat the grill or broiler so that it is very hot. Grill for 3 to 5 minutes on each side, and serve with a knob of butter on the top. Salt should not be added while cooking, but the steak should be seasoned with it afterwards.

Serves 1 or 2 people depending on appetite.

FAGIOLI IN INSALATA
(Dried bean salad)

1 lb. (454 g.) dried beans soaked overnight	4 tablespoons olive oil
1 large onion, finely sliced	2 tablespoons white wine vinegar
2 sage leaves or a pinch of dried	salt
	freshly ground pepper

Put the soaked beans in a large saucepan or pressure cooker with enough water to cover, with salt and the sage. Boil and simmer for about 2 hours, or ½ hour if using the pressure cooker. Add more water if it is getting dry. Strain, and while hot pour over the oil and vinegar, add the onion rings, seasoning, and leave to get cold after stirring very well. Add a little more oil if necessary just before serving.

Serves 4.

Annie Oakley ('Annie get your Gun') with Buffalo Bill's Circus, Rome, March 1890. Photographer, Count Giuseppe Primoli.

UOVA ALLA CACCIATORA

The name of the Pincio derives from the Pinci family who had a magnificent palace there, where Belisarius lived in A.D. *537. Originally it was known as the 'Hill of Gardens or Thrushes', the best known being the garden of Lucullus who converted the slopes into a fine series of terraces. It was here that he lived and held his famous banquets of which Plutarch wrote: 'The life of Lucullus was like an ancient comedy, where first we see great actions, both political and military, and afterwards feasts, debauches, races by torchlight, and every kind of frivolous amusement.' Lucullus was the first person to bring cherries to Italy from Asia and his name has passed into history as a great gourmet, his military victories being overlooked. After Lucullus the villa belonged to Valerius Asiaticus and was coveted by Messalina, who had him condemned to death. Later when she had taken possession she held orgies there, and was subsequently herself murdered there, at the command of her husband, the Emperor Claudius.*

The Villa Medici, designed by Annibale Lippi in 1544, belonged to Cardinal Ferdinando de' Medici in 1580. Galileo was imprisoned there from 1630 to 1633 for having declared that the earth revolved around the sun. It was purchased by Napoleon in 1803, since when it has housed the French Academy where many famous French painters and musicians have stayed. Nearby on one of the slopes is the restaurant Casina Valadier, designed by Valadier, Napoleon's architect in Rome. The terrace of this excellent restaurant affords a wonderful panorama of Rome. See also pages 94 and 119.

Eggs Lucullus are part of French classical cuisine, and consist of cocotte eggs on a base of pâté de foie gras, covered with sliced truffles or mushrooms and baked (for about 20 minutes) in consommé flavoured with Madeira. However, the following baked eggs are an Italian speciality.

UOVA ALLA CACCIATORA
(Hunters' eggs)

3 tablespoons olive oil	4 tablespoons dry white wine
1 small onion, finely chopped	1 lb. (454 g.) puréed tomatoes
6 chicken livers	6 eggs
a pinch each of chopped basil	salt
and oregan	freshly ground pepper

Heat the oil and lightly fry the onion until soft, then the chopped chicken livers, until brown outside, but pink in the middle. Season and add the herbs, tomatoes and wine, and simmer for about 5 minutes. Break the eggs, leaving them whole, into this and bake in a hot oven (425°F.) for about 15–20 minutes, until the whites are set. Serve with toast.

Enough for 3 to 6.

The Villa Medici and the Salita del Pincio, Pincio Gardens, c. 1905.

ABBACCHIO ALLA CACCIATORA

Passetto's restaurant, which is situated between the Piazza Sant' Apolinare and the Piazza Zanardelli with nearby the famous Piazza Navona, was first opened in 1860. It still maintains its excellent reputation for good food at reasonable prices, and has both indoor and outdoor dining-rooms. The word passetto *means secret passage and derives from the old passage which connects St Peter's and the Castel Sant' Angelo, where many popes took refuge during the struggles for power against the Papacy.*

ABBACCHIO ALLA CACCIATORA
(Young lamb, hunters' style; see also page 107)
Recipe kindly given by Passetto's restaurant.

4 lb. (2 kg. approx.) young
   lamb, either leg or shoulder
6 tinned anchovies
6 tablespoons olive oil
½ pint (1 cup) (0·285 l.) white
   wine
scant ½ pint (scant cup) (0·285
   l.) white wine vinegar
juice of 1 large lemon

3 large cloves garlic, chopped
1 small hot chilli *or* ¼
   teaspoon chilli powder
2 teaspoons chopped rosemary
1 tablespoon chopped
   parsley
salt
freshly ground pepper

Trim the lamb and cut into small cubes about 1½ inches in size, sprinkle with salt and pepper and the rosemary. Heat up the oil, then lightly fry the garlic, the chopped chilli and the chopped anchovies. Then add the lamb and cook so that it gets brown on all sides very quickly but the middle remains pinkish. Lower the heat, then add the lemon juice and the white wine. Let it come to the boil, cover and simmer gently for about ½ hour or until tender. Finally add the wine vinegar, stir well, cover again and simmer for about 5 minutes. Season to taste and add the chilli powder if not using chilli. Serve at once garnished with the chopped parsley. If you are doubtful about the age of the lamb then simmer for the first time for 45 minutes, checking that the pan does not run dry and adding a little more white wine if necessary.

   Serves 6.

Dining outside Passetto's Restaurant, via Zanardelli, c. 1900.

SPAGHETTI ALL'AMATRICIANA

This piazza is named after the huge stone face and mouth, known as the 'mouth of truth' which is in the portico of the church of S. Maria in Cosmedin. In the Middle Ages it was thought that if anyone told a lie while holding his right hand in the mouth, the fearful stone jaws would shut and cut off their fingers. A brave Englishman did this and was bitten by a scorpion! The church was built in the sixth century to serve the Greek colony expelled from the east by the iconoclasts. The interior is extremely interesting. The Triton fountain was designed by Moratti in 1715.

'. . . the graceful round temple which has long been familiarly called the Temple of Vesta, supposed by Canina to have been that of Mater Matuta, and by others to have been the Aemilian Temple of Hercules alluded to by Festus and mentioned in the tenth book of Livy. It is known to have existed in the time of Vespasian.'

Augustus Hare, Walks in Rome, 1871

SPAGHETTI ALL'AMATRICIANA
(Spaghetti with bacon and onion).

1 lb. (454 g.) spaghetti or noodles etc.	2 tablespoons grated Pecorino cheese or
1 small onion, chopped finely	4 tablespoons Parmesan
1 crushed garlic clove	salt
7 oz. (199 g.) streaky bacon	

Cook pasta according to recipe on page 96, and drain well. While it is cooking cut the bacon into narrow strips, then cook it with the onion and garlic over a medium flame until golden. Then remove the garlic and pour this sauce over the pasta with the cheese, mixing well. Serve more cheese separately. Some trattorie add 1 lb. skinned and chopped tomatoes to the sauce, but this is not strictly traditional.

Serves 4.

FETTUCCINE AL DOPPIO BURRO

The simple but good method of serving noodles that made the fortune of Alfredo, the Roman restaurateur.

Cook 1 lb. (454 g.) fettuccine or noodles as on page 96, and drain well. In a pan large enough to hold the pasta put 4 oz. (½ cup) (113 g.) unsalted butter with the drained pasta, over a medium flame. Stir for 1 minute then put in gradually, ½ pint (1 cup) (0·285 l.) thick cream, and 6 tablespoons of grated Parmesan cheese. Do this in thirds, mixing gently after each addition. Season with a pinch of nutmeg and white pepper. The stirring should be of the gentlest kind; preferably lifting the pasta up with two forks, so that it becomes well-coated, is the best method.

Serves 4 to 6.

Piazza della Bocca della Verità, with Triton fountain, and the so-called Temple of Vesta in background, c. 1890s.

Pecorino

'. . . and the fierce herdsmen, clad in sheepskins . . . The aspect of the
desolate Compagna in one direction, where it was level, reminded me of an
American prairie.'

Charles Dickens, Pictures From Italy, 1845

PECORINO
(Sheep cheese)

Some of the best cheeses in Italy are made from sheep's milk, and
known collectively as *pecorino* or *pecora*. There are many varieties
of it and this hard, salty sheep's-milk cheese is used in country
districts instead of Parmesan, although it is excellent to eat with
black olives and coarse red wine. The Romans are particularly
fond of *pecorino*, as are the Abruzzesi. The Abruzzi have traditionally
supplied Rome with cooks and waiters for many years, and
Spaghetti all'Amatriciana (page 12) from the village of Amatrice
in the Abruzzi has now become a traditional Roman dish.

Excellent sheep cheeses are made in farmhouses on the hills
outside Rome which are only sold locally. *Pecorino Romano* can
weigh up to 25 lb. and is matured for several years before sale.

Ricotta (see page 41) is strictly speaking a soft unsalted ewe's
milk cheese, much loved by the Romans and used in cooking as
well as being eaten with sugar and cinnamon. *Ricotta* is also salted
and smoked and makes a pleasant soft, country cheese.

Caciotto is made from both cow's and sheep's milk in the Marche
and from sheep's milk only in Umbria and Tuscany. Another
delicious sheep cheese from Umbria and Tuscany is *Raviggiolo*.
Provola di pecora comes from the south and is made with sheep's
milk instead of buffalo's or cow's milk. All these local cheeses
should be tried if possible for they will not disappoint. The market
in the Campo dei Fiori (page 29) always has an excellent selection
of these little-known cheeses.

An Abruzzese custom which is popular in Rome is to eat a
juicy pear with sheep's milk cheese: the combination is delicious.

Roman shepherd on the Campagna Romana, c. 1890. Photograph attributed to F. P. Michetti.

TROTE COI FUNGHI

'TROTE COI FUNGHI'

'The Ponte S. Angelo is the Pons Aelius of Hadrian, built as an approach to his mausoleum, and only intended as such, as another public bridge existed close by . . . the statues of S. Peter and S. Paul, at the extremity, were erected here by Clement VII in 1530 and the angels (from Bernini's design) by Clement IX in 1688 . . . Dante saw the bridge of S. Angelo divided lengthways by barriers to facilitate the movement of the crowds going to and from St. Peter's on the occasion of the first jubilee, 1300. [This he records in the Inferno, xviii 29.] The Castle of S. Angelo was built by the Emperor Hadrian as his family tomb, because the last niche in the imperial mausoleum of Augustus was filled when the ashes of Nerva were laid there.'

Augustus Hare, Walks in Rome, *1871*

From about A.D. 423 it was turned into a fortress and was several times besieged by the Goth invaders. Later on it was used as a prison for many famous people including Cellini. The history of the mausoleum in the Middle Ages is almost the history of Rome. The castle gets its name from an occurrence during a penetential procession led by Pope Gregory the Great in A.D. 590. Rome was in the grip of a dreadful plague and Gregory the Great was leading a procession offering up prayers for it to end, when he saw a vision of the Archangel Michael on what was left of Hadrian's tomb, and from then on the plague subsided. A statue of the archangel dominates the castle.

The most interesting way to approach the castle is from the Via dei Corridori and the Borgo S. Angelo, which is one long street bordering on the passetto *that connects the Vatican palace with the castle. This* passetto, *built in the thirteenth century, was used as an escape route by Clement VII, who took refuge in the castle at the time of the sack of Rome in 1527.*

'There is no building in the world that can show so varied and so tragic a history as the Castel S. Angelo.'

Ferdinand Gregorovius, History of Rome in the Middle Ages, *1859–72*

TROTE COI FUNGHI
(Trout with mushrooms)

4 medium trout	2 chopped spring onions *or*
8 tablespoons butter	1 tablespoon chives
4 tablespoons breadcrumbs	6 oz. (170 g.) sliced mush-
salt	rooms
freshly ground pepper	1 lemon

Rub 1 tablespoon butter around a long oven-proof dish and cover with the finely sliced mushrooms. Season well. Put the cleaned fish on top, then pour over 2 tablespoons melted butter and scatter over the breadcrumbs. Dot the top with 2 more tablespoons butter and bake at 375°F. for 15–20 minutes. Meanwhile heat the remaining butter with the onions, add a squeeze of lemon and when foaming, pour over the fish. Serve with wedges of lemon.

Enough for 4.

Fishing on the Tiber in the shadow of the Castel Sant' Angelo, c. 1898.

TACCHINO ARROSTO RIPIENO

Food at race-meetings at the turn of the century was very elaborate compared to today. Turkey is eaten almost all the year round in Italy, and turkey breasts (page 102) can be bought at any small meat or poultry shop. Generally speaking the turkeys in Italy are very small, weighing about 6 to 8 lb., and thus ideal for everyday use.

TACCHINO ARROSTO RIPIENO
(Roast stuffed turkey)

1 turkey, about 8 lb. (4 kg. approx.)	½ cut lemon
4 tablespoons each of butter and oil	1 glass white wine

FOR THE STUFFING

1 lb. (454 g.) minced veal *or* sausagemeat	the chopped liver of the bird
1 lb. chestnuts, boiled and peeled	a pinch of nutmeg
12 prunes, pitted	1 tablespoon butter
1 large pear	salt
2 tablespoons fresh bread-crumbs	freshly ground pepper

Soak the prunes and when they are soft enough, remove the stones. Make a small cut on the chestnuts, then boil them for about ½ hour, and while still warm remove both the skins, then mash them up. Peel the pear and chop it into small cubes, also the liver of the bird. Combine all the stuffing ingredients, mixing them well. Stuff the bird with this mixture and secure with a skewer.

Wipe and dry the bird, then stuff it, and rub all over with the lemon, then the olive oil, a little butter, and salt and pepper. Put into a roasting tin, cover with foil, and roast in a moderate oven (350°F.) for 20 minutes to the pound, lowering the heat to 300°F. after the first 45 minutes. Warm the wine slightly, then baste with this at least twice during cooking. When ready put on to a warmed serving dish and leave covered with the foil for 5 minutes, as this makes carving much easier. Meanwhile, pour off any excess fat, and reduce the gravy on top of the stove, adding a further glass of wine if more is needed. Season to taste and serve separately.

Serves 8.

IL GARAFOLATO

There are still several pensione *and restaurants run by nuns in Rome and in the heat of the summer eating out-of-doors in a shady arbour is delightful. Many of the first-class restaurants such as George's, Via Marche, Casina Valadier on the Pincian Hill, and Passetto's, have terraces for eating outside, as do some of the humbler ones such as Otello alla Concordia, Via della Croce, where a pretty stone fountain increases the feeling of coolness.*

IL GARAFOLATO
(Roman beef stew with cloves)

2½ lb. (1 kg.) lean round beef	½ inch cinamon stick
2 tablespoons olive oil	a pinch of nutmeg
1 medium sliced onion	6 whole cloves
2 cloves chopped garlic	1 cup red wine
salt	3 large peeled tomatoes, or
freshly ground pepper	equivalent can
1 small chopped head of	1 teaspoon chopped parsley
celery	1 cup water

Cut the meat into quite large cubes, then heat the oil and brown them in it. Add the onion and garlic, cut into pieces, and cook until they soften but do not let them brown. Add the cinnamon, nutmeg, cloves and parsley, then pour over the wine and add the tomatoes coarsely chopped. Season to taste, then add the water. Cover and bring to the boil, and simmer over a gentle heat for about 2 hours, or put into a low to moderate oven (300°F.) for

Nuns serving an alfresco meal, c. 1890. Fondo di Principe Chigi.

the same time. Half-an-hour before it is ready, stir well, take out 4 tablespoons of the liquid and add the same of water, then cook the chopped celery in this liquid until tender. Put back into the beef before serving.

Serves 4.

Reserve any liquid for the dish below.

MELANZANA ALLA ROMANA
(Eggplant Roman style)

2 medium or 1 large eggplant	1 can tomatoes, 16-oz. size
3 tablespoons olive oil	6 thin slices of Mozzarella or
2 tablespoons melted butter	Bel Paese cheese
salt	3 tablespoons grated Parmesan
freshly ground pepper	cheese
1 cup meat sauce, or from stew	pinch of fresh basil or oregan
as above	

Peel the eggplants and slice them thinly lengthwise. Then heat the oil and brown on both sides and drain. Take a 3-pint fire-proof dish and pour in the melted butter then add a very thin trickle of the meat sauce, then a layer of eggplant slices, seasoned to taste. Cover with 2 slices of the Mozzarella and a sprinkle of Parmesan mixed with basil, then a trickle of meat sauce and a little chopped tomato. Repeat this, ending with the meat sauce and tomato until all ingredients are used, then bake in a moderate oven (375°F.) for 15–20 minutes.

Serves 4.

CARCIOFI ALLA ROMANA

The Arch of Titus stands on top of the Velia, a spur of the Palatine that juts towards the Esquiline. It was erected in A.D. *81 to commemorate the capture of Jerusalem eleven years previously. It was restored by Napoleon's architect Valadier. See page 9.*

'. . . the Via Sacra passes under the Arch of Titus, which, even in its restored condition, is the most beautiful monument in Rome. Its christian interest is unrivalled, from it having been erected by the senate to commemorate the taking of Jerusalem, and from its bas-reliefs of the seven-branched candle-stick and other treasures of the Jewish temple. In medieval times it was called the Arch of the Seven Candlesticks . . .'

Augustus Hare, Walks in Rome, *1871*

'Standing beneath the arch of Titus, and amid so much ancient dust, it is difficult to forbear the commonplaces of enthusiasm, on which hundreds of tourists have already insisted. Over the half-worn pavement and beneath this arch, the Roman armies had trodden in their outward march, to fight battles, a world's width away. Returning victorious, with royal captives, and inestimable spoil, a Roman triumph, that most gorgeous pageant of earthly pride, has streamed and flaunted in hundred-fold succession over these same flagstones, and through this yet stalwart archway.'

Nathaniel Hawthorne, Notebooks in France and Italy, *1858*

CARCIOFI ALLA ROMANA
(Roman artichokes)

10 young artichokes
2 cloves chopped garlic
10 fresh mint leaves
salt
freshly ground pepper
3 tablespoons chopped parsley

$\frac{1}{4}$ pint ($\frac{1}{2}$ cup) (0·142 l.) olive oil
1 pint (2 cups) (0·57 l.) water *or* half water and half white wine

Take off the hard outer leaves of the artichokes (and if using ones which have been grown in a cold climate, then it is advisable to cut down and scoop out the choke), force open the hearts and stuff with 1 mint leaf and a piece of chopped garlic and a pinch of parsley, all of which have been well seasoned. Put them in a deep heavy saucepan, standing upwards, then add the olive oil and water or wine and water and more seasonings. Cover and cook gently for about 1 hour or until the liquid is reduced by half. Serve them hot or cold with some of the juice.

Allow 2 per person unless very small.

Sightseers in the Roman Forum admiring the Arch of Titus, c. 1890s.

FRITTO MISTO DI MARE

Ostia is an ancient town fourteen miles south-west of Rome, and is now part of the commune of Rome. The Via Ostiensis which leads to it is of very early origin and preserves fragments of the old pavements and the remains of several old bridges. It is said to be the first colony ever founded by Rome, by Ancus Martius, and it took its name from its position at the mouth (ostium) of the river. Cleopatra is said to have landed there when she came to Rome to be Julius Caesar's mistress. In the 4th century B.C. a fort was built there of volcanic stone and this may be the model for Virgil's description of the fortified camp which Aeneas founded at the mouth of the Tiber. Out of this fort the city developed the establishment of the salt-marshes, which only stopped working in 1875. However, the silting up of the harbour even in Augustus Caesar's time made it far from ideal and Portus Augusti, built under the Emperor Claudius, took most of its trade. In the Middle Ages it became a quarry for the cathedral of Orvieto, and it was not until the late eighteenth century that excavations were commenced, the sand preserving the buildings to a remarkable degree.

Its proximity to Rome makes modern Ostia a popular resort for many Romans today.

A Day at Ostia, c. 1895. Fondo di Principe Chigi.

FRITTO MISTO DI MARE
(Mixed fried fish in batter)

PASTELLA (frying batter)

6 oz. (¾ cup) (170 g.) flour
3 tablespoons olive oil
¾ cup tepid water
pinch of salt
1 beaten egg-white
12 prawns
1 lb. (454 g.) 2-inch chunks of fish (filleted)

½ lb. (227 g.) rings of squid if available
deep oil for frying
lemon
parsley

This batter is particularly crisp and light and can be used for fruit fritters, vegetables, or small pieces of meat and chicken. If any is left over it will keep covered in the refrigerator for a few days, but will not be quite so crisp when fried.

Sieve the flour, then stir in the oil and add the salt and water, stirring until it is a smooth cream, and rather thick. Leave to stand for at least an hour, then fold in the stiffly-beaten egg-white, mixing it so that it gets right down to the bottom. Dip the small pieces of fish into this batter and cook in deep oil on all sides until golden. Drain on paper and serve with wedges of lemon and parsley.

The above batter makes enough for 4 people.

POLLO ALLA CREMA

'. . . at the end of the street, is the Palazzo Mattei, built by Carlo Maderno [during the years 1595 to 1618] for Duke Asdrubal Mattei, on the site of the Circus of Flaminius. The small courtyard of this palace is well worth examining, and is one of the handsomest in Rome, being quite encrusted, as well as the staircase with ancient bas-reliefs, busts, and other sculptures. It contained a gallery of pictures, the greater part of which have been dispersed. The rooms have frescoes by Pomerancio, Lanfranco, Pietro da Cortona, Domenichino, and Albani. The posts and rings at the corner of the streets near the Mattei Palace are curious relics of the time when the powerful Mattei family had the right of drawing chains across the streets during the papal conclaves, and of occupying the bridges of San Sisto and Quattro Capi, with the intervening region of the Ghetto.'

Augustus Hare, Walks in Rome, *1871*

POLLO ALLA CREMA
(Chicken cooked in cream), a rich dish which befits the gorgeous Palazzo.

1 chicken, jointed into serving pieces, about 3–4 lb. (1½ kg.)
1 large lemon
2 tablespoons flour
salt
freshly ground pepper
2 tablespoons butter
1 pint (2 cups) (0·57 l.) cream
1 tablespoon potato flour, or instant potato powder
2 tablespoons brandy

Rub the chicken pieces all over with the cut lemon, then season the flour and roll them in it. Heat the butter in an ovenproof casserole and lightly brown the chicken pieces. Pour over three-quarters of the cream (it should just cover the joints, otherwise add a little more, but reserve some), cover and cook in a moderate oven, 325°F., for about 45 minutes, basting at least once. Take the casserole from the oven and remove the joints and keep warm. Then put the casserole on top of the stove and add the potato flour, moistened with a little water (or dry if using the powder), and stir until it thickens. Add the rest of the cream and the brandy, and bring to just under boiling point, stirring all the time. If it boils it might curdle so be careful. Put the chicken back in the sauce and taste for seasoning. Serve with boiled rice and peas cooked in the Roman way, page 1.

Serves 4.

Courtyard of the Palazzo Mattei, Piazza Mattei (also called Piazza delle Tartarughe), c. 1890. Photographer, Stefano Colisegio.

PESCHE RIPIENE

This colourful market still goes on every morning except Sunday, and it is only then that the statue in the middle of the market, of Giordano Bruno, who was burnt here for heresy in 1600, reminds us the square was a place of execution at that time. Before that it was residential (the Orsini palace dominated the south-eastern end) with at least one well-known inn, La Vacca, owned by Vanozza Cattanei, who after her liaison with the Borgia pope, Alexander VI, ended, shrewdly invested part of her fortune in four inns. In the nearby Vicolo del Gallo at number 13 the shield bearing her arms quartered with those of her third husband and the Borgia pope still survive. Leading from the Vicolo del Gallo is the Piazza Farnese with the magnificent Palazzo Farnese (the French Embassy since 1871 but open to the public for an hour on Sunday mornings), built by Alessandro Farnese (later Pope Paul III, 1534–49), which was designed by Sangallo until his death in 1546, when Michelangelo took over; the work was finally completed by Giacomo della Porta in 1589. Also in the vicinity are the Palazzo della Cancelleria and the Palazzo Spada.

Put the peaches in boiling water for 2 minutes, then peel off the skins. Cut in half and remove the stones, also a little of the flesh which should be put into a separate bowl. Mix the flesh with all the ingredients except the wine, brandy and icing sugar, but see that the macaroons are well pounded so that they resemble crumbs. Stuff the peaches with this mixture, spreading it over the halves. Put into a fireproof dish then moisten each one with the brandy, dust with icing sugar and pour the wine around. Bake in a moderate oven (350°F.) for about ½ hour. Serve either warm or cold with their own juice.

Serves 4 to 6.

PESCHE RIPIENE
(Stuffed peaches)

8 large peaches not too ripe
5 macaroons (or double if small)
2 tablespoons sugar
1 tablespoon chopped candied peel

1 glass white wine
2 tablespoons brandy or Cointreau
2 tablespoons icing (confectioner's) sugar

Fruit and vegetable stall in the Campo dei Fiori, c. 1890. Photographer, Count Giuseppe Primoli.

FLORENTINES

From the late eighteenth century the Caffè Greco was a favourite meeting place for German painters, writers and composers, so much so that the poet Johann Henise suggested that it should be called Caffè Tedesco (German café). Humperdinck first came to Italy in 1879, when he was awarded a Mendelssohn scholarship. There, he met Wagner, also an habitué of the caffè, who invited him to assist in the Parsifal at Bayreuth. Perhaps his most well-known work is the opera Hänsel und Gretel which he wrote in 1893. The Caffè Greco has the most delicious biscuits and cakes and excellent tea and coffee as well as stronger drinks. The little cakes given below are likely to be found there. See also pages 4 and 54.

FLORENTINES

8 oz. (1 cup) (227 g.) butter
6 oz. (¾ cup) (170 g.) caster sugar
4 tablespoons whipped cream
8 oz. (1 cup) (227 g.) blanched almonds cut into very fine strips

4 rounded tablespoons flour
2 heaped tablespoons chopped candied peel (orange and lemon)
2 heaped tablespoons chopped glacé cherries

FOR THE COATING
8 oz. (227 g.) dark chocolate

Heat the butter and sugar gently and when it has melted add the cream very lightly beaten, stir well and let it boil for about 1 minute. Mix in all the other ingredients, except the coating, and stir very thoroughly. Grease a large baking sheet and drop little heaps of the mixture on to it, with a teaspoon, very far apart as they will spread in cooking. Bake in a moderate oven, 350°F., for about 10 minutes or until they are golden brown around the edges. Remove from the oven, let them cool a little then ease them off with a palette knife and put on to a wire tray to get cold.

Meanwhile melt the chocolate for the coating very gently on a plate over boiling water, and when the cakes are cool spread the flat side only with the chocolate and draw wavy lines down it with a fork. Leave until quite cold and dry, then serve with the chocolate side downwards. They can be made any size but the smaller ones are pleasant to eat with tea or coffee as they are quite rich.

Makes about 40.

Engelbert Humperdinck, the German composer, with his wife and family at the Caffè Greco, Via Condotti, c. 1898.

PIZZA RUSTICA

This aqueduct, together with the Anio Novus, was started by Caligula in A.D. 38 and completed by Claudius in A.D. 52. The springs of Claudius were situated near the 38th milestone of the Via Sublacensis, and according to Frontinus over ten miles of the water course were above ground, and seven miles from Rome it united with the Novus, following a natural isthmus formed by a lava stream from the Alban volcano, upon a line of arches which still forms one of the most conspicuous features of the Campagna.

'. . . saw the Claudian aqueduct and three of its branches one of which came to the Palace of the Caesars . . .'

Samuel Rogers, The Italian Journal, *1821*

PIZZA RUSTICA
(Rustic pizza)

FOR THE PASTRY

6 oz. ($1\frac{1}{2}$ cups) (170 g.) self-raising flour

3 heaped tablespoons butter, or lard and butter mixed

a pinch of sugar and salt

4 tablespoons cold water

FOR THE FILLING

1 heaped tablespoon butter or margarine

1 heaped tablespoon flour

1 pint (2 cups) (0·57 l.) warm milk

2 eggs, separated

1 cup each of grated Parmesan and Bel Paese cut into dice

3 tablespoons Ricotta or cottage cheese

1 cup chopped ham

4 slices chopped salame

2 tablespoons sultanas

1 chopped hard boiled egg

a pinch of nutmeg

salt

pepper

Make the pastry in the usual way, then let it rest for $\frac{1}{2}$ hour. Turn out on to a floured board and roll to fit a 10 inch pie-dish. Lightly grease the dish and put the pastry over it, pressing down the edges very well. Brush over with a little beaten egg-yolk.

Make the filling by melting the butter and stirring in the flour, then add the warmed milk and stir until it is quite smooth. When cooled, add the egg-yolks, mixing well, and all the other ingredients except the egg-whites. Finally beat the egg-whites until fairly stiff and fold them in. Put the filling into the pastry dish, roll out the remaining pastry pieces and cut into strips to form a lattice across the pie, and put them over, first damping the edges well and pressing down. Bake in a moderate oven (350°F.) for about $\frac{1}{2}$ hour, or until the pastry is golden and the filling set. This pizza is excellent eaten cold, and also served just warm, not hot.

Serves 6.

Enjoying a day at the Aqueduct of Claudius, Campagna Romana, c. 1868. Photographer, P. Molins.

CARCIOFI ALLA GIUDIA

Piperno's in the Ghetto was founded by Pacifico Piperno in 1860 but has now passed to the Mazzarella family. It is a first-class restaurant set in the tiny Piazza de' Monte Cenci, overlooked by the Palazzo Cenci where lived the notorious Francesco Cenci who was murdered at the behest of his two children, Beatrice and Giacomo, the story of which is immortalized in Shelly's 'The Cenci'. Monte dei Cenci is formed by the ruins of the Circus built in 221 B.C. by Gaius Flaminius the Censor, and nearby in the Via San Bartolomeo dei Vaccinari was the birthplace of the Roman Tribune Cola di Rienzi, the son of an innkeeper and a washerwoman.

Jewish history in Rome goes back a long way: the first Jewish slaves were brought to Rome by Pompey the Great, but for centuries afterwards they lived in Rome in honour, their princes Herod and Agrippa being received with royal distinction. The Jews were first shut up in the Ghetto by Pope Paul IV. Gates in the walls, which reached from the Ponte Quattro Capi to the Piazza del Pianto, were closed at night, and this practice was only abolished in the early years of Pope Pius IX, and freedom was restored to the Jews after the establishment of a united Italy in 1870.

The ancient Romans were said to have found the artichoke in Judea, the name being *kharshûf*, becoming *carciofo* in Italian, and they became inordinately fond of it. The Roman countryside grows the tenderest and most succulent artichokes and *carciofi alla giudia* is the Jewish way of cooking them. Piperno's is called 'the home of the artichoke cooked the Jewish way' but they have many other excellent specialities including *fritto misto vegetariano*, which is an assortment of vegetables and zucchini flowers fried in the batter given on page 25. For other artichoke recipes see page 22.

CARCIOFI ALLA GIUDIA
(Globe artichokes the Jewish way)
Recipe kindly given by Signor Mazzarella.

Only the youngest artichokes should be used for this dish, which when cooked resembles a bronze sunflower. Take medium sized, tightly closed artichokes and put them in cold water for 2 hours. Then cut the stalk, but leave about 2 inches: take off the outside leaves, and holding the artichoke by the stalk, cut off the tips with a sharp knife. Sprinkle with salt and pepper, then press them down on a board so that they flatten a little. Have ready a deep pan (traditionally earthenware) of very hot oil, then plunge the artichokes in, stalk upwards. Turn over and around with a wooden spoon, or tongs, for about 10 minutes. Return them to original position, stalk uppermost and press down gently so that the leaves spread out.

Put them on to a hot plate and shake a few drops of cold water over to crisp them up. Cut off the stem with scissors and serve at once. When cooking for the first time do one or two at a time and keep them warm.

Allow 2 per person.

Piperno's artichoke float on Carnival Day, c. 1920.

FUNGHI

The variety of mushrooms available in Rome, indeed all over Italy, is a delight. The *porcini*, or boletus, is the most common; it is known as *cêpe* in France, a thick, fleshy mushroom which tastes almost like meat. The nearest to them in this part of the world is the large field mushroom, which has the same texture when cooked. If these are not available then use the largest cultivated mushrooms for the following recipes, the small button mushrooms are only good for specific recipes or for serving raw, sliced very thinly and served with an olive oil and vinegar dressing, or seasoned cream.

FUNGHI RIPIENI
(Stuffed mushrooms)

12 large mushrooms	2 tablespoons freshly grated
4 rashers bacon or ham	Parmesan cheese
2 small chopped garlic cloves	2 tablespoons breadcrumbs
2 tablespoons chopped parsley	4 tablespoons olive oil
1 tablespoon butter	salt
	pepper

Chop up the bacon or ham, also the parsley and the garlic: trim the mushrooms of stalks, chop the stalks and add to the bacon mixture. Add the Parmesan cheese and the breadcrumbs. Put the large mushrooms into a well-buttered baking tin and divide the above mixture over them, season to taste and dribble the oil evenly over the lot, adding a little more if the mushrooms are extra large. Cover with a sheet of foil and cook in a moderate oven (350°F.) for about ½ hour. Check that the mushrooms are not drying up; if necessary add a little more oil to each one.

Serves 4 to 6.

FUNGHI CON PIGNOLE
(Mushrooms with pine-nuts)

12 large mushrooms	freshly ground pepper
3 tablespoons butter or olive oil	2 oz. (½ cup) (57 g.) pine-nuts
2 tablespoons chopped	or chopped, blanched
parsley*	almonds
salt	1 large, chopped garlic clove

Slice the mushrooms if they are large, that is over 2 inches in diameter, otherwise leave whole. Heat up the butter or oil until hot and put in the garlic clove, followed by the mushrooms, and cook for not longer than 3 minutes. Scatter the pine-nuts and parsley over the top and mix well. Season, and cook for a further 4–5 minutes on a very low flame, so that the mushrooms are soft but in no way crisp.

Serves 4 to 6.

* Mint can be used instead of parsley if preferred.

Mushrooms cut into thick slices and cooked in the batter on page 25 are extremely good served either on their own or as an accompaniment to meat or poultry.

Mushroom seller outside a trattoria, c. 1895. Photographer, Count Giuseppe Primoli.

FILETTI DI SAN PIETRO COI CAPPERI

'Out over the great balcony stretches a white awning, where priests and attendants are collected, and where the pope will soon be seen. Below, the piazza is alive with moving masses. In the centre are drawn up long lines of soldiery, with yellow and red pompoms, and glittering helmets and bayonets. These are surrounded by crowds on foot, and at the outer rim are packed carriages filled and overrun with people, mounted on the seats and boxes. What a sight it is! – above us the great dome of St. Peter's, and below, the grand embracing colonnade, thronged with masses of living beings.'

W. Wetmore Story, Roba di Roma, 1870

By tradition the first church which existed on or near the site of St Peter's was the oratory founded before A.D. 90 by Anacletus, bishop of Rome, who is said to have been ordained by St Peter himself. Thus it marks the site where many Christian martyrs suffered in the circus of Nero and where St Peter was buried after his crucifixion. In 306 Constantine the Great began the erection of a basilica, working on it himself, and of this basilica only the crypt remains today. At Julius II's command Bramante destroyed the old building and it was said by James S. Ackerman that 'Almost every major architect in sixteenth-century Rome had a hand in designing St. Peter's'. Michelangelo not only designed the dome but also the main body of the church: Bernini designed the colonnade, and the great bronze Baldacchino above the papal altar in 1633. The church was dedicated by Urban VIII on 18th November 1626 and the building extended for over one hundred and seventy-six years altogether.

'The piazza, with Bernini's colonnades, and the gradual slope upwards

Benediction in Piazza di San Pietro (St Peter's Square), c. 1888.

to the mighty temple, gave me always a sense of having entered some millennial new Jerusalem . . .'

George Eliot

FILETTI DI SAN PIETRO COI CAPPERI
(Fillets of John Dory with capers)

Other thick white fish such as sole, bass, turbot, etc. can also be used.

4 fillets of John Dory	salt
3 tablespoons butter, unsalted if possible	freshly ground pepper
	1 tablespoon chopped chives
2 tablespoons coarsely chopped capers	or green onions
	1 tablespoon chopped parsley
1 lemon	flour

Roll the fillets in flour, then heat up 1 tablespoon butter and when foaming fry the fillets on both sides until golden brown and cooked through. Season and put on to a warmed serving dish. Heat up the rest of the butter, add the capers, chives and parsley, also the juice of half the lemon. Just heat through then pour over the fillets and serve with more lemon juice.

Fennel is good with fish: see page 52.

GNOCCHI

GNOCCHI ALLA ROMANA
(Semolina dumplings with cheese)

There are several kinds of gnocchi, one being made with potato and thought to originate in Piedmont: they can also be made with ricotta (a skim-milk cheese made from either sheep, goat or cow's milk, but cottage cheese can be used) and flour. These light little dumplings make an excellent luncheon dish or a first course.

4 oz. (113 g.) semolina (if the fine kind is used then you may need another table-spoon)	6 tablespoons grated Parmesan cheese
	a good pinch of nutmeg
	salt
1 pint (2 cups) (0·57 l.) milk	pepper
yolks of 3 eggs or 2 whole eggs	4 tablespoons butter

Bring the milk to the boil and season it with the nutmeg, salt and pepper. Pour in the semolina in a thin stream, stirring all the time until you have a thick mixture in which the spoon will stand up. This will take about 15–20 minutes until the semolina is properly cooked and firm. Let it cool to tepid, then stir in the egg yolks or eggs and half the cheese. Turn out on to a cold surface and when quite cold and solid cut into rounds about 1½ inches in diameter. Well butter a fireproof dish and put in a layer of gnocchi, then melt the rest of the butter and pour it over with half the remaining Parmesan. Repeat this process until the gnocchi are used up also the butter and cheese. Heat up in a moderate oven (350°F.) for about 10–15 minutes and serve hot. The cheese in the dish should be enough without serving any separately. If liked a small amount of chopped ham (4 slices) can be added when the eggs and cheese are put in.

Serves 4.

GNOCCHI DI RICOTTA
(Cottage cheese gnocchi)

Mix together ½ lb. (227 g.) ricotta or cottage cheese, 2 tablespoons butter, 4 tablespoons grated Parmesan cheese, 2 eggs, 3 table-spoons flour, salt, pepper and nutmeg. Form into small cork shapes and roll them in flour, then poach gently in boiling, salted water for about 5 minutes or until they rise to the top. Serve hot with butter and grated cheese. They can be made in advance and heated gently, but they are very light and delicious and better eaten straight away after making.

Serves 2 to 4.

1 cup puréed spinach added to the above mixture, the eggs separated, the beaten whites added last, make excellent spinach gnocchi.

Enjoying the evening sunshine, possibly Trastevere, c. 1890.

GRANITA

GRANITA AL CAFFÈ
(Coffee granita)

Recipe kindly given by Signor Grimaldi.

Granita is a water-ice, very easy to make and very refreshing in hot weather. It can also be made with lemon juice or fresh, sieved soft fruits.

6 tablespoons finely ground coffee

4 tablespoons sugar

2 pints (4 cups) (slightly over 1 litre) water

1 cup cream freshly whipped (optional)

Put the coffee and sugar into a large jug and pour over the boiling water, then stand the jug in a saucepan of hot water with a very low flame underneath and let it infuse for about ½ hour, but on no account let it boil.

Remove from the heat and let it get cold, then strain it through the finest mesh so that no grounds remain. Pour into 2 refrigerator trays approximately 11½ × 4½ × 1½ inches and put into the freezing compartment for about 2½–3 hours. Half way through freezing, when it is mushy, turn it out into a bowl and beat very well with a fork, then return to the trays and continue freezing until it is of sherbet consistency.

Serve in tall glasses (the texture will be quite mushy or 'grainy') with a blob of fresh cream on top if liked, although for thirst-quenching it is better without the cream.

Serves 6.

GRANITA DI LIMONE
(Lemon granita)

½ pint (1 cup) (0·285 l.) lemon juice

4 oz. (½ cup) (113 g.) sugar

1 pint (2 cups) (0·57 l.) water

First make a syrup by boiling together the water and sugar for 10–15 minutes, then leave to get cold. When cold add the lemon juice and freeze as above.

Serves 6.

Sieved raspberries or strawberries (1 lb. (454 g.)) can also be used instead of lemon juice.

'Lemonade with snow in it. How much more elegant than our ice.'

Samuel Rogers, *The Italian Journal*, 24th January 1821

Signorina Gubinelli (later Signora Grimaldi, and present owner of the Caffè Greco) pours coffee for her governess and the younger members of her family, on the balcony above the Caffè, Via Condotti, c. 1900. See also pages 5, 30, 54.

ROGNONI RIPIENI

'Close by the old Curia was the Basilica Porcia, built by Cato the Censor, which was likewise burnt down at the funeral of Clodius. Near this the base of the rostral column, Colonna Duilia, has been found. Beyond this, on the left, are the remains of the Temple of Antoninus and Faustina, erected by the flattery of the senate to the memory of the licentious Empress Faustina the Elder, the faithless wife of Antoninus Pius, whom they elevated to the rank of a goddess. Her husband, dying before its completion, was associated in her honours, and the inscription, which still remains on the portico, is "DIVO ANTONINO ET DIVAE FAUSTINAE EX. S.C." The façade is adorned with eight columns of cipollino [Marmor Curystium from Euboea, called cipollino from its layers, like an onion], forty-three feet high, supporting a frieze ornamented with griffins and candelabra. The marble steps and coating of the walls were removed as material for the Fabbrica di San Pietro in 1540.'

Augustus Hare, Walks in Rome, 1871

ROGNONI RIPIENI
(Stuffed kidneys, adapted from a recipe of Apicius in the first century A.D.)

12 large lamb's kidneys	pepper
3 tablespoons chopped pinoli (pine-kernels)	a pinch of ground fennel-seed
	4 tablespoons olive oil
2 tablespoons chopped fresh coriander* or	1 teaspoon Worcestershire sauce
1 tablespoon chopped parsley and thyme mixed	2 tablespoons mushroom ketchup
	1 teaspoon soy sauce

* Fresh coriander, although difficult to buy, is easy to grow from seeds. Crush them very slightly, then plant in a box of prepared soil and keep watered. In less than two weeks the plants will appear and they will be ready for cutting in another three weeks. The taste is quite unlike that of the seeds, resembling a very strong orangey parsley, and makes a good addition to kidneys, liver or pork dishes.

Trim the kidneys of any fat and skin them, then cut in two but leave them joined together, and remove the fatty core. Stretch them out and press down the middles. Mix well together the nuts, pepper, coriander and ground fennel seed. Put a small amount into each kidney and fold up, securing with a cocktail stick or small skewer. Heat the oil (use half if the pan is small, and cook half the kidneys first) then quickly brown the kidneys all over. Put them into a roasting dish and add the sauces to the pan juices, stirring well. Pour this mixture over the kidneys and bake in a hot oven, 400°F., for about 20 minutes.

Serves 4 to 6.

Sightseers at the Temple of Antoninus and Faustina in the Forum, c. 1845. Photographer, W. H. Fox Talbot.

SALTIMBOCCA

This gay little fountain in the Piazza Mattei, which houses the Palazzo Mattei (page 27), is off the Via dei Funari, named from the funari or rope-makers, who worked there. The Fountain, which is made of bronze, was executed by Taddeo Landini, probably to the design of Giacomo della Porta, in 1585, and is so full of life and gaiety that even in a city as beautiful as Rome, one constantly returns to it.

SALTIMBOCCA

which means literally 'jump into the mouth', seems an apt dish to accompany this photograph. Although originally from Brescia, it is so popular in Rome that it has become a Roman speciality.

8 slices of thin veal about 4
    inches square
8 slices the same size of raw or
    cooked ham
2 tablespoons butter

8 fresh sage leaves
$\frac{1}{4}$ pint ($\frac{1}{2}$ cup) (0·142 l.)
    Marsala or white wine
salt
freshly ground pepper

Put the veal between two sheets of waxed paper and beat until it is as flat as possible. On each slice lay a slice of ham and a fresh sage leaf. Roll them up and secure with a cocktail stick. Heat the butter until it is foaming then fry them gently until they are golden brown all over. Pour over the wine and let it come to the boil, then cover and simmer very slowly for about 10–12 minutes or until the veal is tender when lightly pricked with a fork. Taste the sauce for seasoning before serving. Small new potatoes with butter and parsley, or slices of bread fried in butter make good accompaniments for this dish.

    Serves 4.

BABINGTON'S SCONES

In 1893 Miss Anna Maria Babington, a descendant of the Catholic Anthony Babington who was executed for leading a conspiracy against Queen Elizabeth, and Miss Cargill, whose ancestor was 'The Fighting Parson', Donald Cargill, an ardent Protestant, also executed for treason in 1681, opened Babington's Tea Rooms in the Via dei Macelli. Rome was full of British people longing for their cup of tea and the following is an extract from the Roman Herald, December 1893:
'A long felt want in Rome has at last been supplied, and that is a tea-room where ladies or gentlemen, hard at work sightseeing . . . could go to refresh themselves with a comforting cup of tea or coffee . . . a quiet read of the best English, Italian and foreign daily papers . . . a tidy up and a good warm.' There was also a reading room for which a modest fee of 10 centimes was charged.

In 1894 they also opened tea-rooms in the Piazza di San' Pietro, but this lasted only about six months. In 1896 they moved to the present premises in the Piazza di Spagna where both the quality and the decorations remain almost unchanged. The tea is excellent, small tins (with the famous Babington cat on them) of the five different varieties are sold, and as well as English and Scottish cakes, light meals of good quality are sold. Miss Cargill married the painter Count da Pozzo (page 3) but continued to work with Miss Babington until she retired in 1928. Their daughter, the Contessa Dorothy Bedini, now runs the restaurant which I hope will continue for many more years. The multi-lingual staff are particularly kind and helpful and have been there for years.

'Thank God for tea. What would the world do without tea? How did it exist? I am glad I was not born before tea.'
Sydney Smith, English cleric, writer and wit, 1771–1845

BABINGTON'S SCONES
Recipe kindly given by the Contessa Bedini.

1 lb. (4 cups) (454 g.) flour	½ lb. (1 cup) (227 g.) currants
3½ oz. (½ cup) (100 g.) sugar	or sultanas
3½ oz. (½ cup) (100 g.) butter	3 coffee spoons baking powder
or margarine	¼ pint (½ cup) (0·142 l.) milk
3 eggs	to mix

Mix the flour, sugar, and currants together, then work in the fat with the hands. Beat 2 eggs with the baking powder and ¼ pint (or 4 tablespoons) milk, then stir into the flour mixture and mix thoroughly. The paste should be fairly stiff but malleable. Turn out on to a floured surface and roll out to a thickness of 1 inch, then with a small cutter, 1½ inches across, cut into rounds. Put on to a lightly greased baking sheet, beat the remaining egg and brush over the tops, then bake in a hot oven (400°F.) for 15 minutes or until the tops are golden.

Makes approximately 24.

Miss Cargill in Babington's Tea Rooms, Piazza di Spagna, 1897.

STRACCIATELLA

Since the seventeenth century the Piazza di Spagna has been the centre of the foreign colony in Rome, and although it was known as the 'English Ghetto' by Romans, it has also housed many other foreigners. Many fashionable streets such as the Via Condotti (pages 4, 54) lead off it, and there is hardly a visitor of note from all over the world who has not stayed there, or nearby. Keats died on 23rd February 1821 in the house on the right (now a museum), one window looking over the beautiful steps and the other over the Barcaccia fountain. This fountain was designed by Bernini's father and as the water from the Acqua Vergine would not rise to any height, he designed it in the shape of a boat (the old barge) that would rest on the water. It commemorated the flood of 1624 when the Tiber overflowed and left a boat stranded at the foot of the Pincian Hill.

The steps are named after the Spanish Embassy in the piazza, but they would more aptly be called the French steps as they were first thought of by Louis XIV, and 24,000 scudi was left by a French diplomat, Étienne Gueffier, for a chapel in the Trinità dei Monti and a staircase leading up to it. They were finished in 1725. The Trinità dei Monti was built in 1495 by Charles VIII of France, run by the French order of the Sacred Heart nuns, who still sing vespers as they did in Mendelssohn's time. It contains many exceptional paintings, particularly Daniele da Volterra's 'Descent from the Cross'. The Villa Medici (see page 8) in the shady Viale della Trinità dei Monti, houses the French Academy. When Goethe was in Rome in 1787 the obelisk at the top of the steps had not yet been built. He wrote in his diary Italienische Reise: 'They were digging up the ground on the Trinità dei Monti for the new obelisk. All around is broken masonry, in what were once the gardens of Lucullus . . .' He found a flat piece of clay with figures on it: 'I eagerly secured the treasure . . . it is not quite a hand long and seems to have been part of a great key . . . I am uncommonly delighted with my new acquisition'.

STRACCIATELLA
(Roman egg soup)

A delicious, nourishing soup, possibly enjoyed by Keats during his last illness. The following is for one person. Beat up 1 egg in a basin with 1 teaspoon of fine semolina, 1 tablespoon grated Parmesan cheese, a small pinch of nutmeg and 1 teaspoon of parsley. Have ready 1 large cup of good seasoned stock, either chicken or beef (a cube will do), and mix 2 teaspoons with the egg mixture. Heat up the rest of the broth and when nearly boiling, slowly pour the mixture into it, beating with a fork; or whisk for 3 minutes. The egg mixture should be in small flakes. Serve at once.

The Spanish Steps, Piazza di Spagna, leading to the Trinità dei Monti, with the house where Keats died on the right, c. 1860. Photographer, D'Alessandri.

MAIALE UBRIACO

'. . . Wine-carts going into Rome, each driven by a shaggy peasant reclining beneath a little gipsy-fashioned canopy of sheepskin . . .'
Charles Dickens, Pictures from Italy, *1845*

Rome is perhaps unique in that it is a capital city with many vineyards in its immediate vicinity: the wines of Frascati, Albani, Grottaferrata and others are of excellent quality.

MAIALE UBRIACO
(Drunken pork)

4 pork loin chops	1 teaspoon chopped rosemary
½ lemon	or powdered oregan
salt	¼ pint (½ cup) (0·142 l.)
pepper	chianti or other red wine
1 tablespoon oil	

Trim the chops of bone and fat, then rub them with cut lemon, salt and pepper. Heat up the oil and then add the chops, browning them quickly on both sides and adding a little of the herb to each chop, on both sides. When the chops are sealed of their juices add the red wine, cover and simmer very gently for about 20 minutes, turning over at least once, until the meat is cooked. Most of the liquid will have been absorbed during cooking, but if it runs dry then add another 2 tablespoons of wine so that there is enough in the pan to make a sauce. Pour this over the chops when serving.
Serves 4.

FINOCCHI
(Fennel)

is very good with this dish: it can either be served raw, cut in thin strips, plain, or mixed with diced cucumber or radishes, and dressed with olive oil flavoured with lemon juice or white wine vinegar: or cut into rings and fried in the pastella, page 25; or cooked as for celery. Fennel also makes an excellent gratin.

FINOCCHI GRATINATI

3 medium fennel bulbs	¾ pint (1½ cups) (0·42 l.) warm
2 heaped tablespoons butter	milk
2 tablespoons flour	3 tablespoons freshly grated
salt	Parmesan cheese
pepper	3 tablespoons crisp breadcrumbs

Clean and cut the fennel into halves or quarters, and cook them in boiling salted water for about 15 minutes, then strain. Make the sauce by heating the butter, adding the flour, then the milk, stirring until smooth. Season to taste and add the cheese. Put it over the fennel in an ovenproof dish, and cover the top with breadcrumbs. Bake for 20 minutes in a moderate oven (350°F.) until the top is browned.
Serves 4.

Bringing the wine to Rome, 1890.

RICOTTA AL CAFFÈ

The first record of the Caffè Greco goes back to 1760 in a census which is kept in the church of San Lorenzo in Lucina, giving the Greek owner's name. However, it had been there for some years before that and is mentioned in Casanova's Memoires in 1742. In the 1780s the French painter Prud'hon wrote about it as a known meeting place in a letter to his friend Fauconnier, and in 1779 Goethe and his friends Tischbein and Moritz were regular customers. But the nineteenth century saw the golden age of the caffè, when every well-known writer, painter and musician, as well as colourful figures such as King Ludwig I of Bavaria and Lord Byron, went there. Gogol used to draw scenes of the Roman Campagna on the marble table tops, and it was here that Hans Andersen (who at one time lived above the caffè) was introduced to Elizabeth Barrett Browning in 1861, by the American sculptor, W. Wetmore Story. The house opposite provided well-known lodgings for the English: Tennyson, Thackeray and Joseph Severn, the poet Keats's friend, all lived there.

The appearance of the Caffè is unchanged since 1860 and on the walls hang paintings and medallions by such artists as Angelica Kauffman, Massimo d'Azeglio and many others. It is still a true caffè, comfortable and elegant, with excellent service. See also pages 5, 30, 43.

In the eighteenth century this area around the Piazza di Spagna (page 50) was known as the 'English ghetto', and all foreigners, whether English or not, were described so – and ennobled, an expression of the time being: 'Milordi pelabili ottimi clienti' – 'Milords easily fleeced and the best customers'. Other caffès in the vicinity were the Caffè Inglese, frequented by rich foreigners; Caffè Ruspoli, by young men about town; and the Veneziano in the Piazza Sciarra patronized mainly by archaeologists and clerics, but also by musicians such as Rossini and his friends. The Caffè Italia is also mentioned in diaries of the period, but alas the only survival is the Greco.

RICOTTA AL CAFFÈ
(Cream or cottage cheese with coffee)

Sieve ½ lb. (2 cups) (227 g.) ricotta or cottage cheese, and mix into it 2 tablespoons freshly-roasted, pulverized coffee (or instant), 4 tablespoons rum and 6 tablespoons caster (extra-fine) sugar. Stir until it is smooth. Leave to stand for at least 2 hours in a cold place, then serve in glasses with wafers.

Enough for 4.

It can also be made with pulverized chocolate.

54

Chess players at the Caffè Greco, Via Condotti, c. 1890.

LIMONATA

Bibitari are small kiosks which sell iced fresh citrus fruit drinks, usually oranges or lemons cut up with the juices squeezed and served in a glass with crushed ice. They still exist in parts of Rome, particularly in the Ghetto, although the water no longer comes relayed by pipes (as in the photograph) from a nearby fountain. Most of the well-known fountains in Rome had the purest water relayed directly from Agrippa's aqueduct, the Acqua Vergine *built in 19* B.C. *Legend says that a young girl, possibly called Trivia, first showed its source, which rises near Salone about fourteen miles from Rome, to thirsty Roman soldiers. It is the shortest ancient aqueduct and also supplied the Trevi fountain (page 91) and the Barcaccia Fountain in the Piazza di Spagna (see page 50).*

The Renaissance Fountain in the Piazza della Rotonda is surmounted by a small Rameses II obelisk which was found in the Campus Martius. This piazza was a fish market and also sold live caged birds until 1847.

'*At a few paces from the streets where the meat is sold, you will find gathered around the fountain in the Piazza della Rotonda, a number of bird-fanciers, surrounded by cages in which are multitudes of living birds for sale. Here are Java sparrows, parrots and parroquets . . . and the* aziola *which Shelley has celebrated in one of his minor poems.*'

W. Wetmore Story, Roba di Roma, *1870*

In the street to the east of this piazza is the unique church Santa Maria sopra Minerva, so-called because it was built over a pagan temple to the goddess, about 1280. It contains many art treasures including some beautiful frescoes by Fra Lippo Lippi, and a Michelangelo sculpture of the risen Christ bearing the cross. There are many chapels and tombs to great Roman families and monuments to popes and cardinals, as well as the body of St Catherine of Siena, who died in the nearby Via S. Chiara on the 29th April 1380 in her thirty-third year. 'At length she died worn out by inward conflicts, by the tension of a half-delirious ecstasy, by want of food and sleep, and by the excitement of political life.'

J. A. Symonds's Sketches in Greece and Italy, *1898*

LIMONATA

Take 4 lemons and squeeze the juice from 2 and put into a glass jug. Cut up the remaining lemons into quarters, or eighths if they are very large, then steep them in the juice. Sweeten to taste and add 1 cup of cold water or crushed ice. To serve put crushed ice to half-fill a glass and strain over the sweetened juice.

Serves 4.

Oranges can be served the same way.

56

The bibitari *in the Piazza della Rotonda, c. 1875 (see also page 85).*

CROSTATA DI RICOTTA

'Oh, she thinks there's nothing like Rome.'
Henry James, Daisy Miller, *1877.*

CROSTATA DI RICOTTA
(Roman cheesecake)

FOR THE PASTRY (to line an 8-inch flan tin)

6 oz. (1½ cups) (170 g.) plain
   flour
3 oz. (scant ½ cup) (85 g.)
   butter
2 tablespoons sugar

finely grated rind of 1 lemon
1 egg-yolk
2 tablespoons approx. cold
   water

FOR THE CREAM

2 tablespoons granulated
   sugar
2 egg-yolks
1 heaped tablespoon plain
   flour

scant ½ pint (scant cup) (0·285
   l.) milk

FOR THE FILLING

1¼ lb. (3 cups) (567 g.) *ricotta*
   or cottage cheese
3 tablespoons caster (extra-
   fine) sugar

1 cup chopped candied fruit
3 eggs, separated
a pinch of cinnamon

Miss Miller, Caffè Greco, Via Condotti, c. 1886.

Make the pastry first, by rubbing the butter into the flour and sugar. Then add the lemon rind, the egg-yolk and the water. Do this quickly, knead a little, roll into a ball, cover and leave in a cool place for about ½ hour.

Then make the cream, by mixing together the sugar, egg-yolks and flour over a gentle flame, adding the milk gradually and stirring all the time. Simmer, stirring well for about 5 minutes until it is smooth and well mixed.

Put the ricotta or cottage cheese into a bowl and mash it with a wooden spoon, then add 2 egg-yolks, the sugar and the cinnamon. When the cream is cold mix it into the filling, with the chopped candied fruit, and finally the 3 egg-whites beaten until stiff.

Roll out the pastry on a floured board, reserving a little for the lattice strips later. Grease the flan tin and put on the pastry, pressing the edges down very well and pinching them. Beat the remaining egg-yolk and paint a very little of it over the bottom of the pastry (this prevents it from becoming soggy), then put in the filling. Put into a low oven (300°F.) for 10 minutes.

Meanwhile roll out the remaining pastry and cut it into strips about ½-inch wide. Take out the cheesecake and cover the top with these strips, and brush it all over with the remaining egg-yolk. Put back into a moderate oven (350°F.) for about 45 minutes, then turn off the heat and leave there for half-an-hour. Do not cut it until it is quite cold, but do not chill.

Serves about 6.

PANETTONE

'*Passing these arches we find ourselves facing the Porta Maggiore, formed by two arches of the Claudian Aqueduct. . . . Out-side the gate, only lately disclosed, upon the removal of constructions of the time of Honorius . . . is the Tomb of the Baker Eurysaces, who was also one of the inspectors of aqueducts. The tomb is attributed to the early years of the Empire.*'

Augustus Hare, Walks in Rome, *1871*

The famous Baker's Tomb has a frieze depicting all the stages of breadmaking, from bringing the corn from the mill, to its distribution. The circular holes in the photograph are, in fact round stone ovens. It was erected by Antina the wife of Eurysaces, and nowadays the traffic presents a very different picture from the one in the photograph, which shows how food and wine were brought to Rome formerly.

PANETTONE

Not a bread for everyday, but although originally from the north of Italy, it is eaten at every big *festa*, such as Easter and Christmas. In Italy it is cylindrical in shape, but it is the marvellously light texture that is as important as the shape.

1 packet (2 heaped teaspoons) of dried yeast, *or*	3 beaten eggs
1 oz. (28 g.) of fresh yeast	3 tablespoons seedless raisins
4 tablespoons tepid milk, see recipe	2 tablespoons chopped candied peel
4 oz. ($\frac{1}{2}$ cup) (113 g.) soft butter	pinch of salt
3 tablespoons sugar	1 egg-yolk mixed with 2 tablespoons water for garnish
12 oz. (3 cups) (340 g.) flour	

Dissolve the yeast in the tepid milk, then cream together the butter and sugar. Add the eggs to the butter mixture, then mix the flour and salt together. Put the yeast into the flour, then put in the butter and egg mixture, and add another 4 tablespoons of milk if it appears to be sticking. The dough should be soft, but at the same time firm enough to knead. Turn out on to a floured surface and knead for about 5 minutes, sprinkling your hands with flour to prevent sticking. Put into a warm bowl, cover and leave for 2 hours until it is doubled in size. Knead about, until any air bubbles are gone and until it doubles in size again. Put out on to a floured surface and flatten it out by punching with the knuckles. Then sprinkle the fruit over, fold and flatten the dough and roll at least twice.

Form into a ball, and put into a deep round greased tin, so that it comes to half-way up. Cover again, and let it stay for 1 hour. Preheat the oven to 400°F. Brush the top of the panettone with the egg-yolk beaten with water, put in the oven and cook for 10 minutes, then lower the heat to 350°F. and cook for a further 30 minutes, or until it has puffed up and is golden in colour.

Serves about 8.

ANITRA IN AGRODOLCE

The annual Horse Show in Rome is now held in May in the Piazza di Siena, in the Villa Borghese park. Romans have always loved horses as the many equestrian statues in Rome will testify, and if they drive their motor-cars like chariots, well, they have a long tradition behind them.

Gabriele d'Annunzio, Prince of Monte Nevoso, was born in 1863 in the Abbruzzi of Dalmatian descent, and wrote a highly praised book of poems while still at school. He joined the staff of La Tribuna *in 1883 and wrote under the pseudonym of 'Duca Minimo'. It was on this paper that he did some of his finest work. He was a novelist, poet and soldier, as well as being the lover of many famous and beautiful women, notably Eleanora Duse the Italian, tragic actress. After the First World War he assumed the role of ruler of Fiume, and defied the Italian government for fifteen months. He was a brave and colourful person, who wrote poems of great beauty.*

ANITRA IN AGRODOLCE
(Duck in sour-sweet sauce)

1 duck weighing about 4 lb. (2 kg.)	2 tablespoons chopped fresh mint
2 tablespoons each of butter and oil	
2 large sliced onions	2 tablespoons sugar, heated with ½ cup water, until it turns golden
a pinch of ground cloves or allspice	
1 pint (2 cups) (0·57 l.) chicken or meat stock	2 tablespoons red or white wine vinegar
1 tablespoon flour	1 tablespoon pine-nuts (*pignole*)
salt	1 tablespoon sultanas
freshly ground pepper	

First wipe the duck inside and out, then season with salt and pepper and roll in flour. Heat up the butter and oil in an oven-proof metal casserole and lightly fry the onions until they are soft, but not coloured, then add the duck and brown all over. Shake over the cloves, then add the stock, let it come to the boil, then cover and simmer very gently for 1½ hours, turning from time to time so that it cooks evenly. Take the duck out and keep it warm, then pour off any excess fat from the pan juices, and stir in the mint, pine-nuts and sultanas. Add the caramellized sugar (heated with the water for 15 minutes) and the vinegar and simmer for 10 minutes. Taste for seasoning, and then serve it separately with the duck. This is also excellent served cold, but remove any fat from the top before serving the sauce.

Serves 4.

Pork or chicken can also be cooked the same way.

*Flirtation at the Horseshow (*Concorso ippico*), at the Hippodrome Tor di Quinto, May 1893. In white is the Contessa Maria Gori Mazzoleni for whom Gabriele d'Annunzio wrote 'Lohengrin all'Apollo' in* La Tribuna, *December 1884. Photographer, Count Giuseppe Primoli.*

INVOLTINI ALLA CIOCIARETTA

Many of the travellers of the last century have written about the picturesque models who lounged about on the Spanish Steps (see page 51) and nearby, waiting to be hired by artists. Charles Dickens in Picture from Italy, 1845, writes: '. . . I could not conceive why the faces seemed familiar to me: . . . I soon found that we had made acquaintance, and improved it, for several years, on the walls of various Exhibition Galleries. There is one old gentleman, with long white hair and an immense beard, who, to my knowledge, has gone half through the catalogue of the Royal Academy.'

There were all country people, some from the Campagna, but mainly as in the photograph, from Ciociaria, an area between Rome and Naples. They were called ciociara because they never wore shoes, but sandals (ciocie) like the Roman legions. The women's dress was always a starched head-dress of white linen, and a black velvet bodice worn over a full white blouse. They adorned themselves with gold earrings and coral beads. Some of the models came from the village of Saracinesco high up in the Sabine Mountains and had Arabic names, for they were said to be descendants of a Saracen raiding party cut off in A.D. 927, who were permitted, after renouncing their faith, to stay in the mountains. Not a few of these picturesque figures are still to be seen in Rome.

Ciociaria has produced some very good recipes: Gina Lollobrigida also comes from there.

INVOLTINI ALLA CIOCIARETTA
(Veal slices Ciociaretta)

By kind permission of Mr Vernon Jarratt, owner of George's, Via Marche, one of the finest restaurants in Rome.

1 lb. (454 g.) lean veal cut into slices 3 inches square and ½ inch thick	¼ lb. (113 g.) sliced button mushrooms
6 oz. (170 g.) mozzarella cheese *or* Bel Paese *or* Provatura	4 tablespoons dry white wine or dry sherry
2 wafer-thin slices of raw Italian ham (*prosciutto crudo*), or lean bacon	2 tablespoons butter
	salt
	freshly ground pepper
	a little flour

Beat the veal slices until they are paper-thin, then cut the ham and cheese into strips about one third the size of the veal. Put one of each on to the veal strips towards one end, season lightly and fold into two. Pound the edges to seal them then roll in flour. Heat up the butter until foaming, then cook the veal 'packets' until they are golden on both sides. Pour in the wine and let it all simmer very gently for about 10 minutes, turning them once. Then add the finely sliced mushrooms and cook for 5 minutes. Put the veal on to a warmed dish, then add 2 tablespoons or so of water to the pan, scrape down the sides, boil up and serve over the meat.

Serves 4.

Ciociara 'Costumi' (artists' models), waiting to be hired in the Pincio Gardens, c. 1890s.

SPINACI ALLA ROMANA

Many writers have been deeply moved by the Colosseum, including Lord Byron, Goethe and Dickens. As early as the seventh century the Venerable Bede wrote: '... When falls the Colosseum Rome shall fall, and when Rome falls, the world.' Byron's description is apt today: 'A ruin – yet what a ruin; from its mass, Walls, palaces, half-cities, have been reared.' But perhaps Dickens, writing in the same year as the photograph was taken, expresses both the majesty and the horror which the sight of the Colosseum inspires in most people: 'It is the most impressive, the most stately, the most solemn, grand, majestic, mournful sight conceivable. Never, in the bloodiest prime, can the sight of the gigantic Coliseum [sic], full and running over with the lustiest life, have moved one heart as it must move all who look upon it now, a ruin. God be thanked: a ruin!'

Charles Dickens, Pictures in Italy, *1845*

The building was started in A.D. *72 by the Emperor Vespasian, and originally called the Flavian Amphitheatre: the last two rows were finished by Jewish slaves brought back by Titus after the conquest of Jerusalem, but it was finally completed under Domitian* A.D. *81–96. Fifty-thousand people could be accommodated to watch the spectacle of slaughter, of both human beings and animals. Emperor Commodus (*A.D. *180–92) frequently fought there himself, killing both gladiators and wild beasts. He called himself Hercules, and dressed in a lion's skin with his hair sprinkled with gold-dust. The first martyr was Saint Ignatius, who was eaten by lions, but thousands of Christians, saints and other people perished on this site, in various ways. At least some of the beaten gladiators could appeal to the crowd for mercy, for if they put their thumbs up (a sign meaning* Mitte – *let him go) he was reprieved, but thumbs down meant* Jugula – kill him. *One wonders what the carefully sheltered Vestal Virgins (the only women allowed in the official seats) thought of these 'games'. The last games were held by Anicius Maximus in* A.D. *523, and in the Middle Ages the Colosseum became a place for sorcerers, Cellini experiencing an encounter with devils; also a place for pageants and plays. The romantics of the eighteenth and nineteenth centuries vowed that it should only be visited by moonlight, and after dinner, carriages would draw up for this purpose. Goethe wrote: 'The moon illuminated it like a mist; it was an exquisite moment.'*

SPINACI ALLA ROMANA
(Roman spinach)

To 1 lb. (454 g.) of well-drained cooked spinach, add 1 tablespoon raisins, 2 tablespoons pine-nuts (*pignole*), 1 crushed garlic clove, a pinch of nutmeg and seasonings. Fry this gently in a mixture of 2 tablespoons of butter and oil for about 10 minutes, lifting and stirring it all the time. Add 2 heaped tablespoons of grated Parmesan cheese and mix it through before serving, hot.

Serves 4.

Visitors to the Colosseum, c. 1845. Photographer, W. H. Fox Talbot.

ZUPPA PAVESE

'On the destruction of Jerusalem by Titus, thousands of Jewish slaves were brought to Rome, and were employed on the building of the Coliseum [sic]. At the same time Vespasian, while allowing the Hebrews in Rome the free exercise of their religion, obliged them to pay the tax of half a shekel, formerly paid into the Temple treasury, to Jupiter Capitolinus – and this custom is still kept up in the annual tribute paid by the Jews in the Camera Capitilina.'

Augustus Hare, Walks in Rome, 1871

See also page 35.

ZUPPA PAVESE

This soup was originally from Lombardy, but is now a Roman speciality and found all over Italy. It is a good light meal in itself and excellent for single people or invalids. Not only is it easy to prepare, but it is easy to eat and provides all the nutriment one could want.

Legend has it that it originated in 1525 when Francis I of France was losing the battle of Pavia. He stopped at a farmhouse and asked for food. The farmer's wife, about to serve a broth, added fried bread, egg and cheese. The king was delighted and said: 'What you have given me is a King's soup.' From then on, so the story goes, it was called Zuppa alla Pavese.

1 pint (2 cups) (0·57 l.) stock, either chicken or beef
1 egg
4 small rounds bread
2 tablespoons grated Parmesan cheese
2 tablespoons butter

First heat the butter until it is foaming, then fry the bread until it is just golden brown on both sides, and reserve. Heat up the stock in a shallow pan and when it boils add the egg, whole. It is best to break it first into a cup, then slide it gently in, holding the cup so that it almost touches the broth. Leave to simmer for about 40 seconds, then take the pan off the heat. Lift the egg out with a slice and put into a warmed large soup-plate, then gently pour a quarter of the broth around. Float the bread slices on top and sprinkle half the cheese over them. Pour on the remaining broth and serve with the rest of the cheese to be added as liked.

Serves 1, but if the quantities of stock and bread are increased and more eggs poached it can be made for any number of people. However, it is best to poach the eggs one at a time.

A game of Patience, probably in the Ghetto, c. 1890s. Fondo di Aldo Ravaioli.

TRIPPA ALLA ROMANA

TRIPPA ALLA ROMANA
(Tripe Roman style)

Recipe kindly given by Signor Mazzarella of Piperno's restaurant (Piazza de' Monte Cenci), where it is a speciality.

3¼ lb. (1½ kg.) tripe, preferably veal tripe, and honeycomb	6 tablespoons olive oil
1 large onion	¼ pint (½ cup) (0·142 l.) white wine
1 large clove garlic	1 tablespoon chopped mint
2 sliced carrots	1 can peeled tomatoes, 16 oz.
salt	(454 g.) size
freshly ground pepper	6 tablespoons grated Pecorino
4 stalks celery	or Parmesan cheese

This tripe is very delicious, the fresh mint giving it an excellent flavour. First trim the tripe of any fat, then wash it well in tepid water. Put into a large saucepan, cover with cold water and bring to the boil. Throw off the first water and repeat the operation, then simmer slowly for about 4 hours or until the tripe is quite tender. (Sometimes tripe is sold already half-cooked, in which case simmer for only 2 hours.) Leave it to get cold, then cut it into strips of about 3 inches (7½ cm.).

Fry the sliced onion in the heated oil with the garlic, carrots and celery until they are soft but not coloured. Then season to taste. Add the tripe strips and mix well, letting it heat gently. Pour in the wine and the mint, then let it bubble up and reduce slightly. When it has reduced, add the tomatoes and the juice, mixing it well. Cook again, gently, for three-quarters of an hour. When ready, sprinkle the tripe with the grated cheese, allowing about 1 tablespoon per person, letting it melt a little before serving.

Serves 6 to 8.

Theatre signs in the Corso, 1890. Photographer, Count Giuseppe Primoli.

FAGIANO IN CASSERUOLA

FAGIANO IN CASSERUOLA
(Pheasant casserole; also for guinea fowl, chicken, Cornish rock hens or pigeons)

1 large pheasant
8 juniper berries
2 tablespoons butter
24 seedless white grapes *or*
   the same of muscat raisins,
   seeded
salt
freshly ground pepper
$\frac{1}{4}$ pint ($\frac{1}{2}$ cup) (0·142 l.) dry
   white wine

4 tablespoons Marsala or
   Madeira wine
4 tablespoons brandy
pinch of ground cinnamon
$\frac{1}{4}$ pint ($\frac{1}{2}$ cup) (0·142 l.)
   chicken stock ($\frac{1}{2}$ cube will
   do)

Wipe the bird inside and out then season with salt and pepper, and put the crushed juniper berries into the inside. Heat up the butter in a heavy casserole and brown the bird all over, then add the brandy and flame it before pouring over the stock. Taste for seasoning. Cover and put into a preheated oven at 325°F. and cook for about 30 minutes, then take out, baste (see below) and return to the oven for a further 15–25 minutes or until the bird is tender.

While the bird is cooking make the grape sauce. If using the dried, seeded muscat raisins then soak them in half the wine until they have swollen, then simmer them until tender. If using fresh grapes soak them also in the white wine, add the other wines and the cinnamon and simmer very gently for about 5 minutes, mixing well. Take the pheasant from the oven and baste with this sauce, and leave the casserole uncovered for the extra cooking time given above.

Serves 4.

A halt for refreshments during the shoot, Campagna Romana, c. 1895. Fondo di Principe Chigi.

CRÊPES ALLA RANIERI

On 18th February 1849 Pope Pius IX invited the armed intervention of France, Austria, Naples and Spain to restore his power, which had been removed by the initiation of the Roman Republic, of which Mazzini was made head of the Triumvirate. (At that time Italy was not a sovereign country as it is today but a mixture of small kingdoms and dukedoms.) Thus French forces came to Rome in the mid nineteenth century as defenders of the Papal temporal power against the awakening spirit of democratic nationalism. They remained there until Napoleon III's fall and the victorious attack on Rome by the forces of Italian nationalism, united under King Victor Emanuel II, which took place on 20th September 1870 (see also page 117).

The pretty girl in the photograph had obviously lost her heart to a French soldier and employed the services of a scrivener to translate his letters to her and also so that she could answer them.

CRÊPES ALLA RANIERI
(Pancakes with four cheeses)

Made by the restaurant Ranieri (see page 5). Recipe kindly given by G. Ranieri.

PANCAKE MIXTURE
(for 8 medium pancakes)

4 oz. (1 cup) (113 g.) plain flour	½ pint (1 cup) (0·285 l.) milk
1 tablespoon olive oil	a pinch of salt
1 egg	a knob of butter

FOR THE FILLING

1 heaped tablespoon flour	1 cup Parmesan cheese, grated
1 heaped tablespoon butter	1¾ pints (1 l.) milk
1 scant cup each of: Swiss (Gruyère) cheese, Bel Paese Pastorella*, Fontina	

* Pastorella is a version of Bel Paese but made in smaller sizes: if not available use double quantity of Bel Paese. Fontina is like a rich oozy kind of Gruyère with very small eyes, which is ideal for melting. Other similar cheeses can be found in good delicatessen shops.

First make the pancakes by putting the flour and salt into a mixing bowl, then adding the oil and the beaten egg. Beat well until quite smooth and leave to stand for at least 1 hour. Make the 8 pancakes in the usual way, using a lightly greased hot pan, and rolling about 2 tablespoons of the batter around it so that it spreads evenly and thinly all over. When one side is golden brown then turn, and do the other side. Drain on kitchen paper and leave for stuffing. In a large saucepan melt the butter, add the flour, mix well and let it brown. Then add the cheeses and half the Parmesan and let them melt. When melted add the milk and the rest of the Parmesan and heat, stirring well, until it is thick. Fill the pancakes, roll up and heat in a hot oven (400°F.) until golden.

Serves 4.

The scrivener into French, Piazza Tor dei Specchi (demolished in 1930), c. 1865. From the collection of Ernesto Barberi, Caffè del Teatro Marcello, Via del Teatro Marcello.

PIZZA ALLA CASALINGA

Mount Parioli is now a residential suburb of Rome, consisting of large houses and apartment blocks for the middle and upper classes. It is hard, when looking at this photograph, to resist the temptation to say that workmen have not changed much over the years!

PIZZA ALLA CASALINGA
(Home-made pizza)

Although the pizza is a Neapolitan dish originally, it is found all over Italy today. Many working people lunch on them at a *pizzeria*, and they are popular cold, as a packed lunch. Yeast dough is usually used, but they can be successfully made with baking powder as given below.

FOR THE DOUGH
16 oz. (4 cups) (454 g.) self-
   raising flour
¾ pint (1½ cups) (0·42 l.) half
   milk and half water
2 teaspoons olive oil
1 small boiled potato, mashed
pinch of salt

FOR THE FILLING
1 can tomatoes (16 oz. size)
1 small can anchovies
½ lb. (227 g.) mozzarella
   cheese, or Bel Paese if not
   available
1 teaspoon oregan or basil
2 tablespoons olive oil

Put the sifted flour and salt in a mixing basin, then add the mashed potato, oil, and milk and water. Mix well and knead a little until it is a soft dough. Dust with flour and roll into a ball, cover with a cloth and leave for about 1 hour.

Then cut the dough into 4, oil the baking tray (or use flat tart dishes) put a ball of dough on each, and with the knuckles knead them until they will fit a dinner plate. Separate the anchovy fillets and using half of them divide them between the 4 pizzas, sprinkle oregan over the top, then cover with the drained, mashed tomatoes, distributing them evenly. Cover with the remaining anchovies, then cut the cheese into small pieces and divide this between the pizzas. Trickle a very little oil over each one, and leave for 10 minutes. Then put into a preheated hot oven (425°F.) and cook for 10–15 minutes or until the edges of the pizzas turn golden.

This makes quite a substantial lunch for four people.

Olives can be used instead of anchovies if preferred. Mushrooms (*funghi*), clams or mussels (*vongole*), ham (*peosciutto*), salami, can all be used either with tomatoes, or in the case of mushrooms, without them. The traditional Roman pizza is simply onions, softened until golden in olive oil.

Workmen resting during the levelling of Mount Parioli, c. 1880. Photographer, Ignazio Cugnoni.

BROCCOLI ALLA ROMANA

'The Lateran derives its name from a rich patrician family, whose estates were confiscated by Nero. . . . It became an imperial residence, and a portion of it being given by Maximianus to his daughter Fausta, second wife of Constantine. . . . It was this which was given by Constantine to Pope Melchiades in 312 – a donation which was confirmed to Saint Sylvester, in whose reign the first basilica was built . . . and consecrated in November 324. This basilica was overthrown by an earthquake in 896, but was rebuilt by Sergius III [A.D. 904], being then dedicated to St. John the Baptist.'

Augustus Hare, Walks in Rome, *1871*

It was the original parish church of Rome, and the skulls of Saints Peter and Paul are said to be preserved there. The façade in the photograph was built by Alessandro Galilei in 1736.

The Piazza di S. Giovanni is dominated by the oldest and tallest obelisk in Rome. Dating from the fifteenth century B.C., it originally stood before the Temple of Ammon in Thebes, and was brought to Rome by Constantius II in A.D. 357. The old Pontifical palace also stood there in the sixteenth century before it was destroyed by Sixtus V, and in front of it stood the bronze equestrian statue of Marcus Aurelius (preserved because it was inaccurately thought to be of Constantine), which now stands in front of the Capitol.

BROCCOLI ALLA ROMANA
(Roman broccoli)
This broccoli is a meal for the gods.

2 lb. (1 kg.) flowering broccoli	4 tablespoons olive or cooking
2 cloves finely chopped garlic	oil
½ pint (1 cup) (0·285 l.) dry	salt
white wine	freshly ground pepper

Take off any tough outer leaves from the broccoli and break it up into the flowerlets, and with a sharp knife make a cross in the stem as you would when preparing sprouts. Soak in cold water for about ½ hour, then drain and pat dry.

Heat up the oil in a pan large enough to take all ingredients, and just soften, but do not brown, the garlic. Then add the leaves of the broccoli and finally the flowers. Season to taste, and sauté for about 7 minutes. Add the wine, cover the pan and simmer gently for about 15 minutes, stirring once or twice. Taste for seasoning before serving.

Enough for 4.

Sightseers at the Basilica of St John Lateran, Piazza di S. Giovanni in Laterano, c. 1910.

Bruschetta

BRUSCHETTA

The Italian equivalent of garlic bread, simple to make and extremely good to serve with simple dishes.

Bake thick slices of crusty bread in the oven until they are crisp and golden. Then rub them with cut garlic cloves and pour olive oil over them while they are warm, and serve at once.

It can also be made with thick slices of toast, but the flavour will not be quite the same.

MOZZARELLA IN CAROZZA

means literally 'mozzarella in a carriage' and is a fried cheese sandwich. Mozzarella is a soft cheese made from buffalo milk and must be used fresh. If it is unobtainable then Bel Paese is a reasonable substitute. In Rome, provatura, the Roman version of mozzarella, is often used.

8 thick slices of bread about 3   2 eggs
inches by 2 inches   6 tablespoons oil
4 thick slices of mozzarella or
Bel Paese

Take the crusts from the bread and put a cheese slice between two slices of bread to make sandwiches. Beat the eggs in a deep plate and put the sandwiches to soak in them, turning over once. Leave for about $\frac{1}{2}$ hour so that both sides get well-soaked. It may be easier to break one egg and do two sandwiches at a time if the plate isn't big enough. Press the sandwiches together so that the cheese is well enclosed, then heat up the oil (again use half and fry 2 if the pan is small) and fry them on both sides until golden brown and the cheese melted. Drain on paper and serve at once.

Serves 2 to 4.

Mozzarella or Bel Paese can also be cut into chunks, dusted with flour then dipped in beaten egg and breadcrumbs and fried quickly in hot oil, on both sides. These make mouth-watering snacks with drinks but must be served hot.

Farm workers resting from their labours, Campagna Romana, c. 1890. Fondo di Aldo Ravaioli.

PROSCIUTTO ROMANO

The beautiful Temple of Castor and Pollux with its three remaining Corinthian columns is one of the ancient sacred places in the Forum. It was originally dedicated by Postumius in 484 B.C. to Helen of Troy's brothers, who are said to have brought the news of the victory of Lake Regillus to Rome. This victory ended for ever the hopes of the Tarquin dynasty and was believed to have been won owing to the divine intervention of the twin brothers, statues of whom also adorn the entrance to the Capitol.

The Basilica Julia was begun by Julius Caesar and finished by Augustus, who dedicated it in honour of the sons of his daughter Julia. It was restored by Severus in A.D. 199 and again by Diocletian after a fire in A.D. 282 and finally by the Prefect Gabinus Vetticus Probianus. Basilicas were vast halls largely used for general meeting places, or law courts, and were later used as models for the large Christian churches. This basilica was used as a Law Court and also as an Exchange: judges called Centumviri held their courts, which were four in number:

'Iam clamor centumque viri, densumque coronae
Vulgus: et infanti Julia tecta placent.'

Martial, Ep. vi 38

'Here Suetonius narrates that the mad Caligula used to stand upon the roof and throw money into the Forum for the people to scramble for. The Arch of Tiberius is supposed to have stood near the corner of this basilica.'

Augustus Hare, Walks in Rome, 1871

PROSCIUTTO ROMANO
(Roman Ham)

From the book of Marcus Apicius, a Roman gourmet at the time of the Emperor Tiberius. He died in the first century A.D. Seneca said that after spending a fortune on food and finding himself penniless, he took poison. Throughout the Middle Ages various copies of his manuscripts have been made.

'Boil the ham with plenty of dried figs and three bay leaves. Remove the skin and make criss-cross incisions, which you fill with honey; wrap it in a paste of flour and oil and cover the ham with this. When the paste is baked take out and serve.'

I have made this excellent recipe using 4 lb. (2 kg.) ham with $\frac{1}{2}$ lb. (227 g.) dried figs and 3 bay leaves, allowing $\frac{1}{2}$ hour's simmering to the pound. Make a paste from 4 cups flour with 2 cups oil and enclose the ham, baking for a further $\frac{3}{4}$–1 hour.

Serves 6 to 8.

It is also very good baked with the honey and without the pastry casing.

The Temple of Castor and Pollux, with the Basilica Julia in background, the Roman Forum, c. 1900.

83

ROAST LAMB, KID, OR PORK

Marcus Agrippa built the original Pantheon in 27 B.C. but it was twice burnt, once during the reign of the Emperor Titus and again under Emperor Trajan in A.D. 110. Emperor Hadrian rebuilt the body of the temple between 120 and 124, his love of Greece showing clearly in the architecture. In ancient times the dome was covered with gilded bronze which was plundered by the Byzantine Emperor Constans II in 655, and replaced by lead in the eighth century. In 608 it was dedicated as a Christian church to St Mary and All Saints or Martyrs, with the permission of the Byzantine Emperor Phocas, and it is due to him that it has been preserved through the ages. Urban VIII added the two ugly campanili (shown in the photograph) which were commonly known as 'the asses' ears', but these were removed in 1885. At one time the apse and niches contained statues of Augustus and Agrippa, as well as the seven great gods and goddesses, with Mars and Venus, the protecting divinities of the Julian house, in the places of honour. The statues of the goddesses were adorned with precious jewels, and according to Pliny Venus wore as earrings the two halves of the famous pearl that Mark Anthony took from Cleopatra, after she had drunk its twin, dissolved in vinegar, when Mark Anthony had challenged her to a bet.

Many of Italy's great artists are buried there, the most famous being Raphael, who died in 1520. His friend Cardinal Bembo wrote the following epitaph:

> Ille hic est Raphaello Sanzio, timuit quo sospite vinci
> Rerem magna parens et moriente mori.

'Here lies Raphael: while he lived the great mother of all things [Nature] feared he might outvie her; and when he died, she too feared to die.'

Generally, the ancient Romans liked all their foods to be served with a strong sauce (see page x). However, a simple and very good recipe comes down to us from the first century for roasting lamb, kid or pork.

ROAST LAMB, KID, OR PORK

For a 4 lb. (2 kg.) boned shoulder or leg of meat, mix together 1 tablespoon of coarse salt and 2 rounded teaspoons of freshly ground coriander, and rub all over the inside of the joint, massaging it in well. Roll up the joint and secure with string. Then mix together 3 tablespoons of olive oil with 2 teaspoons freshly ground pepper and rub this over the outside. Roast in a moderate oven (350°F.) for 20 minutes to the pound for underdone meat, or 30 minutes for well done. Baste with ½ pint (1 cup) (0·285 l.) warm red wine.

Serves 6 to 8.

The Pantheon, Piazza della Rotonda, c. *1875.*

BRISAVOLA

The Grand Hotel is one of the six great hotels in the world. It was founded by Cèsar Ritz in 1894 and for the inaugural banquets he brought over Escoffier, then chef at the Savoy in London, to arrange and supervise. Ritz believed that for an hotel to be really great it must be an integral part of the life of the city – a rendezvous for travellers and Romans alike. This atmosphere continues today and there are two excellent restaurants, Le Rallye Room and Le Maschere. The latter specializes in pasta dishes: there are thirty-eight different regional preparations in Le Maschere restaurant. Most of the recipes are closely guarded secrets, but the way of serving Brisavola, the air-cured beef from the Italian Tyrol, is simple and excellent.

BRISAVOLA LE MASCHERE

If Brisavola is not available then use a good quality dried beef, cut in paper-thin slices.

Arrange thin slices of dried beef on a large plate, with sections of fresh grapefruit, without any peel, pith or pips. Add a few leaves of *rughetta* (a spiky, pungent weed which grows around Rome) or use corn salad if *rughetta* is not available. Make a dressing of 1 tablespoon olive oil and the juice of ½ lemon, add a few grains of freshly ground black pepper and pour over. A delicious course for one.

SPAGHETTI BALDUINI

is named after the *maître d'hôtel* of the Rallye Room, and is still a secret, but basically it is spaghetti cooked as on page 96, served with a sauce composed of fresh cream, flavoured with a little fresh tomato, pimiento and garlic. At the last moment very thin strips of deep-fried zucchini are tossed in. They are so crisp they taste like nuts.

ZUCCHINI FRITTE
(deep fried zucchini)

Also good as a vegetable.

Cut 1 lb. (454 g.) small unpeeled zucchini into very thin strips, like tiny french-fried potatoes. Cover with salt and leave for an hour, then drain and pat them dry. Put 3 tablespoons flour into a cloth and shake the zucchini in it, then have ready a pan of deep hot oil and toss them in. They will take about 3 minutes to cook. Lift out with a perforated skimmer and drain. Season slightly before serving.

Serves 4 to 6.

It is worth experimenting with this pasta dish, but the delight is the crisp addition.

PANSOTI AL LATTE DI NOCI

Another speciality. Triangles of pasta (see Ravioli, page 105) are stuffed only with borage leaves, poached and served with a sauce made from 1 cup pounded walnuts, 2 crushed garlic cloves well mixed and beaten with 1 cup olive oil added gradually so that it thickens.

Passing the fountains in the Piazza San Bernardo on the way to the Grand Hotel, Via Vittorio Emanuele, c. 1895. Photographer, Count Giuseppe Primoli.

SALSA AGRODOLCE

'The Arch of Septimius Severus, which was erected by the senate A.D. 203, in honour of that emperor and his two sons, Caracalla and Geta. It is adorned with bas-reliefs relating his victories in the east – his entry into Babylon, and the tower of the temple of Belus are represented. A curious memorial of imperial history may be observed in the inscription, where we may still discern the erasure made by Caracalla after he had put his brother Geta to death in A.D. 213, for the sake of obliterating his memory. . . . It was in front of this arch that the statue of Marcus Aurelius stood, which is now at the Capitol.'

Augustus Hare, Walks in Rome, *1871*

Emperor Septimius Severus was concerned with Britain for most of his reign, and died there and was cremated at York, where he had made his headquarters with his sons and the Empress Julia. In the Spring of 209 he led his army into the wilds of Caledonia, where the Caledonians inflicted great losses, but did not stem the legions. He was the first Roman general to invade this part of Britain.

It was in the Mamertine prison that St Peter is said to have been confined in a dungeon before his crucifixion.

SALSA AGRODOLCE
(Sour and sweet sauce)

Sour-sweet sauce was a great favourite of the ancient Romans and still survives today in many forms. In the book of Apicius (from the first century) it is mentioned as containing 'pepper, mint, pine-nuts, sultanas, carrots, honey, vinegar, oil, wine and musk'. However, the ingredients today vary according to what meat, game or vegetable it is to accompany. See also page 63.

CIPOLLINE IN AGRODOLCE

Sour-sweet button onions can be served hot with pork and other meat dishes: or cold in an antipasto or as an accompaniment to meats.

2 lb. (approx. 1 kg.) button onions	2 tablespoons sugar
	4 tablespoons white or red wine vinegar
4 rashers streaky bacon, chopped	salt
3 tablespoons olive oil	pepper

Boil the onions unpeeled for 10 minutes and when cool, peel them. Heat up the oil and cook the bacon until golden, then add the sugar, onions and when the sugar has melted add the vinegar and season. Stir, and cook for $\frac{1}{4}$ hour gently, until the sauce is syrupy.

Serves 4 to 6.

East side of the Arch of Septimius Severus, the Roman Forum: to left is the Temple of Jupiter Tonans, to the right a portion of the church built over the Mamertine Prison. The Capitol is in the background. 11th June 1841. Photographer, Alexander John Ellis.

SFORMATO DI RISO E CAVOLFIORE

*This baroque, fantastic fountain with its tritons, gods and goddesses, probably gets its name from the three streets (*tre vie*) which meet in the little piazza, one end of which is the huge Palazzo Poli. It was finally finished in 1762 by Niccolo Salvi for Clement XII and was fed from the* Acqua Vergine *(see page 56). Up till the last century there was a superstition that the traveller who drank from the fountain would return to Rome: nowadays the superstition is that you must throw a coin in the fountain to ensure your return. This money (when not taken surreptitiously by street urchins) goes to charity.*

'. . . nature has adopted the fountain of Trevi, with all its elaborate devices, for her own. Finally the water, tumbling, sparkling, and dashing with joyous haste, and never-ceasing murmur, pours itself into a great marble basin . . .

'In the day-time there is hardly a livelier scene in Rome than the neighbourhood of the fountain of Trevi; for the piazza is then filled with stalls . . . chestnut roasters . . . idlers lounging over the iron railing . . . who come hither to see the famous fountain.'

Nathenial Hawthorne, Notebooks in France and Italy, *1858*

'. . . the fountain of Trevi, welling from a hundred jets, and rolling over mimic rocks, is silvery to the eye and ear. In the narrow street beyond . . . Romans round its smoking coppers of hot broth, and cauliflower stew; its trays of fried fish, and its flasks of wine.'

Charles Dickens, Pictures from Italy, *1845*

SFORMATO DI RISO E CAVOLFIORE
(Baked rice and cauliflower)

Recipe kindly given by Mr Vernon Jarratt, owner of George's, Via Marche.

2 cups (approx. ½ lb.) (227 g.) cooked rice	4 tablespoons butter
1 medium size cauliflower	6 tablespoons Parmesan cheese
1 pint (2 cups) (0·57 l.) of white sauce	6 tablespoons breadcrumbs
1 small chopped onion	salt
	freshly ground pepper

Cut the cauliflower into flowerlets and discard any large leaves or stump. Make cuts on the bottom of the stalks as for sprouts. Cook in boiling salted water for 10 minutes, then drain. Heat half the butter until foaming, then lightly fry the onion, add the rice and fry for 5 minutes turning all the time. Butter a fireproof dish and scatter breadcrumbs on the bottom and sides, then fill the dish with layers of rice, cauliflower, white sauce, cheese, dots of butter and seasoning, ending with the cheese. Sprinkle over the remaining breadcrumbs and butter in dabs and bake in a medium oven (350°F.) for about 30 minutes.
  Serves 4.

A lively scene at the Fountain of Trevi, off the Via di S. Vicenzo, c. 1898. Photographer, Count Giuseppe Primoli.

S̶CAMPI

The Massimo d'Azeglio Hotel was founded in 1875 by the Piedmontese great-great-grandfather of the present owner, Angelo Bettoja. It still maintains an atmosphere of the past, and serves some of the finest food in Rome.

SCAMPI ALLA GRIGLIA
(Grilled Dublin Bay prawns or jumbo shrimp can also be used)

2 lb. (1 kg.) raw scampi,	1 large lemon
Dublin Bay prawns or	salt
jumbo shrimp in their shells	pepper
4 tablespoons olive oil	2 tablespoons chopped parsley

Remove the heads and claws of the prawns, and without removing the shells make a small slit down the underneath side of each one. Then rub them well with salt, pepper and olive oil and put them in a grilling pan. Preheat the grill and cook them gradually, basting from time to time with a little more oil. Turn once to make sure that they are cooked through and flatten them down with a rolling pin to make them easier to peel. In all they should not take longer than about 8 minutes. Put on to a hot serving dish, sprinkled with parsley and served with wedges of lemon. This simple method is a most delicious way for very fresh prawns. Eat with the fingers, first squeezing the shells so that they come off easily.

Serves 4.

The dining-room of the Massimo d'Azeglio Hotel, Via Cavour, c. 1900.

SCAMPI CAVOUR

Recipe kindly given by Signor Bettoja, as served at the Massimo d'Azeglio and the Hotel Mediterraneo, Via Cavour, also owned by Signor Bettoja. Sliced truffles are added when in season.

2 lb. (1 kg.) raw scampi,	1 glass dry white wine
Dublin Bay prawns or	½ lb. (227 g.) mushrooms
jumbo shrimp	4 oz (113 g.) chopped tongue
2 eggs	2 teaspoons tomato purée
4 tablespoons seasoned flour	1 large sliced lemon
4 tablespoons butter	parsley

Remove the shells from the prawns, then beat the eggs and put out the flour on a board. Dip the prawns first in the egg then in the flour. Heat the butter and fry each one until golden all over. Put around the edges of a warmed serving dish and keep warm. Lightly fry the mushrooms in the butter, adding a little more if necessary, until they are soft but not crisp, add the tongue and the tomato purée and mix well. Simmer on a very low flame for about 2 minutes then add the white wine. Let it bubble up, then pour at once into the centre of the dish and garnish with parsley and the sliced lemon.

Serves 4.

BUDINO DI CILIEGE

'"*The Pincian Hill*" *is the favourite promenade of the Roman aristocracy. At the present day, however, like most other Roman possessions, it belongs less to the native inhabitants than to the barbarians from Gaul, Great Britain, and beyond the sea . . .*'
Nathaniel Hawthorne, Notebooks in France and Italy, *1858*

'*From the platform of the Pincio terrace the Eternal City is seen spread at our feet and beyond it the wide-spreading campagna till a silver line marks the sea melting into the horizon beyond Ostia.*'
Augustus Hare, Walks in Rome, *1871*

BUDINO DI CILIEGE
(Cherry pudding)

Cherries seem an apt fruit, for Lucullus, who lived on these slopes, brought the first cherries back to Italy from Asia: also they were the symbol and form part of the coat-of-arms of the Medici family who built the Villa Medici, which is nearby (see page 8). Recipe kindly given by Mr Vernon Jarratt.

2 lb. (1 kg.) ripe cherries
6 eggs
½ lb. (1 cup) (227 g.) granulated sugar
1 tablespoon butter
2 lemons
¾ lb. (8 cups) (340 g.) fresh breadcrumbs
¼ pint (½ cup) (0·142 l.) rum

First stone the cherries and put them aside. In a large bowl put 2 whole eggs, 4 yolks, the sugar, grated rind of the lemons and the juice of one of them. Work this with a wooden spoon until you have a smooth, creamy and fluffy mixture. This can take a little while, but can be done in an electric mixer; if using one, however, then add the lemon rind when it is mixed.

Pour the rum over the breadcrumbs and let it soak for a little while, then add this to the mixture. Beat the egg-whites to a stiff foam then gently fold them in.

Butter a fireproof dish that holds about 5 pints (3 l.) and put an inch layer of the mixture in the bottom, then a layer of cherries. Repeat this until all ingredients are used up, using the mixture as the last layer. Put into a moderate oven (350°F.) for 1 hour, and leave the pudding for 10 minutes before turning out. It can be eaten hot or cold.

Serves 6 to 8.

I have made this delicious pudding using two-thirds the quantity of breadcrumbs, and the remainder of ground almonds. It makes a slightly heavier sweet, but is excellent. Other soft fruits such as raspberries or strawberries can also be used.

Promenade in the Pincio Gardens with panorama of Rome, c. *1865*.

SPAGHETTI ALLA CARBONARA

The Atrium Vestae, as it was called, has been recomposed from the ruins discovered in the autumn of 1883, after the fire of A.D. 191 by Septimius Severus and Julia Domna. 'Under the Alban system, the care of the sacred fire has been entrusted to four virgins; Servius Tullius raised the number to six, which number remained unchanged till the fourth century of the Christian era, when it was increased to seven.'

Augustus Hare, Walks in Rome, *1871*

The Vestal Virgins were chosen at the early age of about seven and lived in great austerity, but also great privilege, the abbess enjoying one of the highest positions under the empire. They all had precedence over everyone except the Empress, and the highest in the land had to make way for their carriages. Criminals were reprieved simply by their intercession and secrets of state and wills were entrusted to them. Yet, if they foreswore their thirty-year oath of chastity they were entombed alive: but after the thirty years they were free to marry. Part of their sacred duties consisted of cooking special salt cakes, called Mola salsa, *used in sacrificial ceremonies, and they rekindled the sacred fire annually on 1st March by rubbing pieces of wood together.*

SPAGHETTI ALLA CARBONARA
(Spaghetti with bacon and egg sauce)

Carbonara means that it was originally cooked over charcoal. It is one of the best pasta dishes, the eggs coating the long strands of spaghetti so that it is creamy and delicious.

1 lb. (454 g.) spaghetti; noodles or tagliatelle can also be used
6 rashers of streaky bacon
2 eggs
1 tablespoon cream (optional)
4 oz. (1 cup) (113 g.) grated Pecorino or Parmesan cheese
1 tablespoon oil
salt

Put 3 quarts (12 cups) water into a large saucepan and bring to the boil. Add a good tablespoon of salt and the oil (this stops the pasta from clumping together), then when it is on a rolling boil add the spaghetti, broken in two if preferred. Stir at once with a large fork, and lower the heat when it comes to a rolling boil again, but do not turn it too low. Cook for about 10–15 minutes; the pasta still will be what the Italians call *al dente,* that is, bite-able. When ready strain in a colander.

Meanwhile, chop up the bacon, and beat the eggs. Wash and wipe round the saucepan that the pasta was cooked in, then put the bacon in it and cook until the fat is melted and it is beginning to crisp. Add the spaghetti, mixing well, and put the flame very, very low. Add the beaten eggs and stir well, then add 4 tablespoons of the grated cheese and cream if using and mix that well too. Take off the heat and stir so that all the pasta is coated by the egg and cheese, then serve with more cheese separately.

Serves 4.

Sightseers at the ruins of the House of the Vestal Virgins, the Forum, 1881. Photographer, Mr Robertson.

POLLO ALLA ROMANA COI PEPERONI

'We now enter the Trastevere, the city "across the Tiber" – the portion of Rome which is most unaltered from medieval times, and whose narrow streets are still overlooked by many ancient towers, gothic windows and curious fragments of sculpture. The inhabitants on this side differ in many respects from those on the other side of the Tiber. They pride themselves upon being born "Trasteverim", profess to be the direct descendants of the ancient Romans, seldom intermarry with their neighbours, and speak a dialect peculiarly their own.'

Augustus Hare, Walks in Rome, *1871*

The Trasteverini are not unlike the London Cockney, or the Montmartois, and probably just about as mixed in blood, for it was the original port of Rome and had a very polyglot community. However, they do have their own dialect, and also a special festa *held in July called* Noiantri *which combines an ancient and modern carnival. The exquisite church of S. Maria in Trastevere in the piazza of the same name is reputed to be the oldest in Rome, the original building having been dedicated to the Virgin Mary in the fourth century; the church of S. Cecilia in the Piazza di S. Cecilia, with its beautiful enclosed garden, should also be seen.*

There are a number of good restaurants in Trastevere, one being Romolo, Via di Porta Settimiana, where Raphael is reputed to have first seen his voluptuous model and mistress, the baker's daughter, 'La Fornarina', in the garden, which is now a grape-covered arbour, delightful to eat in.

POLLO ALLA ROMANA COI PEPERONI
(Roman chicken with peppers)

A speciality of Romolo's restaurant.

1 large chicken, jointed	freshly ground pepper
1 lb. (454 g.) mixed green, yellow and red sweet peppers	1 small, chopped garlic clove
	a pinch of chopped rosemary
	4 tablespoons olive oil
1 lb. (454 g.) ripe tomatoes or equivalent canned	½ pint (1 cup) (0·285 l.) chicken stock (or a cube dissolved)
salt	

Wipe the chicken pieces so that they are dry, then season them lightly. Heat up 1 tablespoon of oil and put all the peppers in and cook over a high flame until they blister all over, then take off the heat and let them cool. Peel off the outer skin, cut them into quarters and remove the seeds and core, then cut into strips. Peel the tomatoes by putting them in boiling water for 2 minutes, then chop or sieve them. Heat up the remaining oil and sauté the chicken pieces until golden all over, then add the tomatoes and peppers, mixing well. Season to taste, add the chopped garlic and rosemary, and also the stock. Cover and either simmer gently on top of the stove for 1 hour, or put into a moderate oven (325°F.) for the same time.

Serves 4.

Trastevere, 'the city across the Tiber', c. 1900.

TORTONI

The Chigi family have a distinguished history which includes two popes, Alexander VII and Clement XII. In the church of Santa Maria del Popolo, the Piazza del Popolo, with its magnificent paintings, is the Chigi chapel, designed by Raphael for his patron and friend the Sienese banker Agostino Chigi. Raphael conceived the chapel, with its heavenly blue and gold mosaics, almost as a separate church inside the larger one. Raphael's work may also be seen in the exquisite Villa Farnesina, built by Baldassare Peruzzi in Trastevere for Agostino Chigi, where he entertained the famous people of the early sixteenth century. It contains some of the most beautiful ceilings, and Raphael's fresco of Galatea, of which Samuel Rogers said in 1820: '... it wins upon you the more you look at it', and much later the great Bernard Berenson wrote: 'Tell me, has she not imparted a thousand times more life and freedom and freshness since you have seen her painted by Raphael in the midst of her Tritons and sea-nymphs?'

TORTONI
(Ice-cream made with macaroons)

The Italians introduced ices to Europe, for Buontalenti, one of Catherine de'Medici's cooks, in 1533 delighted the French court with his iced confections, then unknown in France. A Sicilian, Francisco Procopio, opened the first café in Paris in 1670 for the sales of ices, but cream ices appeared only with Tortoni, an Italian who opened a most celebrated café in Paris at the end of the eighteenth century. This ice-cream is his invention.

2 stiffly-beaten egg-whites
1 pint (2 cups) (0·57 l.) heavy cream
6 tablespoons icing (confectioner's) sugar
pinch of salt
1 cup (½ pint size) macaroons, rolled into crumbs
1 tablespoon rum
2 tablespoons toasted unsalted almonds, chopped

Beat the egg-whites until stiff, gradually adding the icing sugar, about 1 tablespoon at a time. Soak the crumbled macaroons in half the cream, with the rum. Whip the remaining cream until thick with the salt, then fold it into the macaroon mixture. Finally fold in the stiffly-beaten egg-whites and pack the mixture into 10 to 12 plated paper cups about ¼ pint (0·142 l.) size. Decorate the tops with the slivered almonds then freeze until firm.

Serves 8.

FILETTI DI TACCHINO AL MARSALA

The column which dominates this piazza was found on the Monte Citorio in 1709, having been originally erected to the Emperor Marcus Aurelius in A.D. 174. The bas-reliefs which surround it commemorate Marcus Aurelius's victories over the Marcomanni. A statue of the Emperor on top of the column was replaced by the existing one of St Paul in 1589. The Palazzo Chigi (see page 101) is in this piazza and the large building in the photograph, which is now offices of the newspaper Il Tempo, *was the Palazzo Wedekind, built in the last century, but incorporating columns found during excavations in the old city of Veii. In the eighteenth century the column was surrounded by stoves where the whole supply of coffee for Rome was roasted, but by the nineteenth century only the* bibitari *(see page 56) remained and smart caffès were built where the fashionable people driving along the Corso in their carriages stopped for refreshment.*

FILETTI DI TACCHINO AL MARSALA
(Turkey breasts with Marsala)

4 turkey fillets, from the breast	4 tablespoons Marsala wine
2 tablespoons butter	4 tablespoons chicken or
3 tablespoons seasoned flour	turkey broth

Flatten the turkey fillets by banging them slightly with a rolling pin, then roll them lightly in seasoned flour. Heat up the butter until it is foaming and fry them on both sides until golden, about 3 minutes on either side. Add the Marsala and when it is bubbling, add the chicken or turkey broth and cook, uncovered, for about 3 minutes, turning once.

Serves 4.

Turkey fillets can also be fried as above, then on top of each fillet put a layer of sliced mushrooms which have literally just been softened in butter – they must not be at all crisp. Then add a thin slice of, preferably, Fontina cheese, but if it is not available then use either Gruyère or Port Salut. Over each fillet pour a spoonful of chicken or turkey stock, then cover the pan, and on a low flame cook for about 5–7 minutes. The cheese should be melted and amalgamated with the butter. It should be served before the cheese is allowed to become hard and stringy.

Chicken breasts or escalopes of veal can also be used for both these recipes.

CAROTE AL MARSALA
(Carrots with Marsala)

Sauté 1 lb. (454 g.) sliced carrots in a little butter for 2 minutes, then add a glass of Marsala. When it bubbles add enough water to barely cover and seasonings, put the lid on and simmer until they are tender and the liquid reduced.

Piazza Colonna with bibitari, c. *1900.*

PASTA

Pasta is the staple diet of many Italians and the *sfoglina*, a woman who makes pasta by hand, is still very common in Italy. A pasta machine is needed to make spaghetti and other shapes, but the following recipe given to me by Kenneth Macpherson's cook, Antonio (who also cooked for Norman Douglas the writer), is easy to make and excellent for ravioli, lasagne or cannelloni.

TO MAKE PASTA FOR RAVIOLI

A durum flour is the best to use, and if you see a packet with 'pura semola di grano duro', this does not mean semolina, but a hard wheat flour, which is the one used in Italy.

½ lb. (2 cups) (227 g.) plain flour	approx. ½ pint (1 cup) (0·285 l.) boiling water
2 oz. (¼ cup) (57 g.) butter	extra flour for rolling out the
a pinch of salt	pasta

Mix the butter into the salt and flour until it resembles fine bread-crumbs, then add the boiling water, to make a stiff dough. Add either a little more water or flour according to the stiffness of the dough. Knead it slightly, cut into two if making ravioli, and roll out on to a well-floured board or table. It is important to have a space large enough to be able to roll out the dough very thinly in one piece. If this is not possible then roll it in quarters. Sprinkle the pasta continually with flour to prevent it from sticking, and it should be as thin as you can roll it without its cracking or tearing. Keep the pasta that is not being rolled covered with a cloth, and have another handy to cover the rolled one, to prevent cracking when filling. Cover both sheets of pasta and leave for at least 10 minutes before filling.

FILLINGS for ravioli can vary a lot: a popular one is ½ lb. (2 cups) (454 g.) ricotta (or cottage cheese) sieved, then mixed with 3 tablespoons grated parmesan or pecorino, a pinch of nutmeg, 3 tablespoons cream, 3 egg-yolks and a pinch of either basil or marjoram. Mix well, then put about 1 teaspoon at a time on the pasta about 1½ inches apart, and place the other sheet of pasta loosely over the top. Dampen the edges and lines of filling (or paint with egg) and press down well so that the little squares do not come open. Cut down with a sharp knife or a pastry cutter and put the prepared ravioli in one layer *only*, covered with a floured cloth until ready for use. They will keep 2 days. Poach a few at a time in 4 quarts (4 l.) salted boiling water. They will rise to the top when ready; lift out with a slotted spoon and serve with melted butter and grated cheese. Cooked chopped meat, puréed spinach with ricotta as above, can also be used.

Makes about 50 ravioli.

See also page 86.

Women washing at a trough, Campagna Romana, c. 1888.

AGNELLO AL FORNO

'The Capitoline was the hill of the kings and the republic, as the Palatine was of the Empire. . . . Up to the time of the Tarquins, the hill bore the name of Mons Saturnius, from the mythical king Saturn, who is reported to have come to Italy in the reign of Janus, and to have made a settlement here. . . . Under Tarquinius Superbus, B.C. 535, the magnificent Temple of Jupiter Capitolinus . . . was built with money taken from the Volscians in war. In digging its foundations the head of a man was found, still bloody, an omen which was interpreted by an Etruscan augur to portend that Rome would become head of Italy. In consequence of this . . . has ever since been Mons Capitolinis, or Capitolium.'

Augustus Hare, Walks in Rome, *1871*

'The street ends in the sunny open space at the foot of the Capitol, with Ara Coeli on its left, approached by an immense flight of steps, removed hither from the Temple of the Sun, on the Quirinal, but marking the site of the famous staircase to the temple of Jupiter Capitolinus, which Julius Caesar descended on his knees, after his triumph for his Gallic victories.'

Ibid.

The church of Ara-Coeli was built on the site of the Temple of Juno Moneta (which housed an early Roman mint, and it is from this that the word money originated) with the Temple of Jupiter and an imperial palace nearby, and it was here that the sacred geese gave the alarm, thus saving Rome from the surprise attack by the barbarians. The church houses the 'Bambino', a gaudy, jewel-bedecked image of the Child Jesus said to be made from olive wood of the Garden of Gethsemane, which is carried around to the dying and at Christmas is put in the middle of the crib.

The Piazza Ara-Coeli with the Capitol in the background, c. 1900.

Edward Gibbon, after listening to the monks singing vespers in the Ara-Coeli church in 1764, wrote: 'The idea of writing the decline and fall of the city first started to my mind.'

AGNELLO AL FORNO
(Roast lamb)

The true Roman speciality is *abbacchio* which is unweaned lamb, but this is difficult to obtain outside Italy. The following marinated lamb is extremely good.

4 lb. (2 kg.) leg of lamb	4 tablespoons olive oil
1 bay leaf	½ pint (1 cup) (0·285 l.) red
1 sprig rosemary	wine
a pinch of savoury or thyme	1 tablespoon wine vinegar
2 cloves unpeeled garlic	salt
1 teaspoon crushed coriander	freshly ground pepper
seeds	

Marinate the lamb in all the other ingredients except the salt, rubbing it well in, and turning every so often, for at least 2, but preferably 4, hours. Put into a roasting tin with the marinade and roast at 350°F. for 25 minutes to the pound for underdone meat and 30 for medium done, basting at least twice. Salt just before serving and remove the meat to a warm dish, then reduce the gravy over a hot flame, adding a little more red wine if necessary.

Serves 8.

POLLO ALLA ROMANA

Count Primoli was a remarkable photographer at the end of the last century and the beginning of this, and many examples of his spontaneous work will be found in this book (see Contents list). He also took many photographs of Venice and people and places in Paris. His Mother was a Buonaparte and the Fondazione Primoli in Rome houses many Napoleonic treasures.

POLLO ALLA ROMANA
(Chicken in the Roman way)

1 medium size jointed chicken	freshly ground pepper
5 tablespoons olive oil	$\frac{1}{2}$ teaspoon chopped rosemary
1 thick slice diced bacon	$\frac{1}{2}$ teaspoon chopped tarragon
1 large clove chopped garlic	$\frac{1}{4}$ pint ($\frac{1}{2}$ cup) (0·142 l.) dry
$\frac{1}{2}$ pint (1 cup) (0·285 l.)	white wine or vermouth
chicken stock	2 teaspoons tomato purée *or*
salt	4 peeled ripe tomatoes

First rub the chicken joints all over with olive oil, salt and pepper. Then in an ovenproof dish (preferably iron) heat up the rest of the oil, add the diced bacon and the garlic and let them all soften, but not brown, for a few minutes. Add the chicken joints and let them get golden brown on both sides. If the oil seems excessive, then spoon out a little, before adding the chopped herbs and the wine or vermouth. Let this simmer until it is reduced by half, turning the joints meanwhile.

Stir in the tomato purée, or the coarsely chopped tomatoes, and add the chicken stock, which has been warmed. Mix all together thoroughly, then cover and either simmer very gently on top of the stove, or put into a moderate oven (325°F.) for about 40 minutes. The liquid should not be excessive; if it is so at the end of this time, remove the chicken to a warmed serving dish and reduce the sauce slightly on top of the stove.

Serves 4 to 6.

Young, tender green peas are excellent with this dish.

PISELLI ALLA LATTUGA
(Peas cooked with lettuce)

Only very small peas can be used for this dish. These tiny peas were brought to France for the first time in 1660 from Genoa and presented personally to Louis XIV. They became the rage of the court, and even in 1696, when they were being cultivated in France, Madame de Sevigné wrote: 'There are ladies, who having supped, and well supped, with the King, go home and there eat a dish of green peas before going to bed . . . it is a fashion, a fury . . .'

Put 3 cups of young peas into a bowl with 4 tablespoons of soft butter, and mix it well with your hands. Add a pinch of sugar, then line a saucepan with young lettuce leaves, add 2 chopped spring onions, the peas and 1 cup water. Cover with foil and a lid and when boiling lower the flame and cook for 10 minutes.

Serves 4 to 6.

Count Giuseppe Primoli and friend in front of the Arch of Septimius Severus in the Roman Forum, c. 1898.

ESTINI

This train ran from Rome to the enchanting town of Frascati in the Alban hills, a distance of about fourteen miles. It was here that after the death of Charles Edward Stuart (Bonnie Prince Charlie), the Cardinal Duke of York proclaimed himself Henry IX of England. The Vatican did not recognize him, and only his servants, a few Irishmen and those who hoped for favours, addressed him as 'Your Majesty'. The old castle-like palazzo is interesting with its ancient flight of narrow steps, known as the Via Duca di York. Frascati is also famous for its excellent white wine, Cannellino di Frascati.

'On the steep above it the ruins of Tusculum, where Cicero lived and wrote, and adorned his favourite house (some fragments may yet be seen there), and where Cato was born.'

Charles Dickens, Pictures from Italy, *1845*

Not everyone was pleased to have the railway in Rome. Mrs Craven (1808–91) in Anne Séverin *says: 'Those who arrive at Rome now by the railway, and rush like a whirlwind into a station, cannot imagine the effect which the words "Ecco Roma" formerly produced when, on arriving at the point in the road from which the Eternal City could be descried for the first time, the postillion stopped his horses, and, pointing it out to the traveller in the distance, pronounced them with that Roman accent which is grave and sonorous as the name of Rome itself.'*

CESTINI
(packed meals)

are available at most large stations in Italy today, but really the most exquisite train meal consists of paper-thin slices of raw Parma ham (*prosciutto crudo*), crusty rolls (the kind made in Rome are like rosettes and aptly called 'rosetta'), olives, cheese and wine, followed by some excellent Roman fruit. What more could one ask?

However, the Supplì (page 113) also make delicious and filling mouthfuls.

The inauguration of the first train between Rome and Frascati, 1857.

SUPPLÌ

There are still many street musicians all over Italy and many an open-air evening meal is accompanied by a serenade from one or another little band. The quality of the music varies, but it will be a sad day when this old custom is gone for ever.

'A guitar and violins – always moving along –'

Samuel Rogers, The Italian Journal, 1821

SUPPLÌ
(traditional Roman rice croquettes)

These croquettes are very good for a first course or a light luncheon. They are made from left-over risotto or boiled rice and it is well worth cooking extra so that you have some over to make these delicious little mouthfuls. They used to be sold as snacks almost everywhere in Rome and they revive the flagging sightseer's spirits, for further excursions. Several varieties are made, some with meat or sausage and others with cheese, called *Supplì al telefono*, because the melted cheese inside stretches like telephone wires:

3 cups of cooked rice
2 eggs
6 heaped tablespoons breadcrumbs
pepper

12 slices, 2 inches across, of
   mozzarella or Bel Paese
   cheese
6 tablespoons approx., olive oil

Mix together the rice and the beaten eggs, then take about 1 tablespoon of the rice in your hand and flatten it. Lay the slice of cheese on top, then put the same amount of rice over it. Roll into a ball so that the cheese is quite enclosed, then roll gently in breadcrumbs. Do this until all ingredients are finished, then chill for ½ hour.

Heat up the oil and fry them gently so that they become golden brown all over. It is easier to do only two or three at a time, then drain them on kitchen paper. The cheese inside should be just melted, so that it stretches when cut. Makes about 12 croquettes, enough for 4.

Slices of ham can also be added, or used without the cheese in the croquettes: also pieces of mortadella, salami, pastrami, or chunks of meat from a beef stew. They are excellent eaten hot, but also very good served cold or tepid.

Street musicians in Rome, c. 1890. Photographer, Count Giuseppe Primoli.

BIGNÉ

BIGNÉ DI SAN GIUSEPPE

St Joseph's *beignets* are a Roman speciality, always eaten on St Joseph's (patron of hearth and home) Day, but also throughout the year.

Recipe kindly given by Mr Vernon Jarratt.

3 oz. ($\frac{3}{4}$ cup) (85 g.) plain
  flour
2 eggs plus 1 extra egg-yolk
$1\frac{1}{2}$ heaped tablespoons
  unsalted butter
$\frac{1}{2}$ teaspoon granulated sugar

$1\frac{1}{2}$ cups cold water
finely grated rind of $\frac{1}{2}$ lemon
salt
1 pint (2 cups) (0·57 l.) oil
1 cup vanilla sugar* for
  garnish

* Vanilla sugar is fine sugar which has had vanilla pods immersed in it for at least 1 week, but preferably longer. The sugar then becomes delicately flavoured with it.

Put the water, butter and a pinch of salt in a pan over a high flame, and when it boils, tip in the flour, all at once. Work it well with a wooden spoon, keeping it over the flame, until it is a ball which easily leaves the sides of the pan. Take off the stove and let it cool a little.

Add, one at a time, the 2 eggs and the extra yolk, mixing well with the wooden spoon for about 10 minutes until it is quite creamy. This is done off the stove. Add the $\frac{1}{2}$ teaspoon of sugar and the lemon rind and work again for 5 minutes. Let it all rest in a cool place for 45 minutes.

Have ready 2 teaspoons, dipped in hot water, then put the oil into a pan and when it is *tepid* add some of the *bigné*, having shaped them with the 2 teaspoons to about the size of a hazelnut. Raise the flame to high and fry the *bigné* until they have swollen up and become pale gold in colour. Do not overcrowd the pan: it is easier and better to do a few at a time. Drain them on kitchen paper and sprinkle them with the vanilla-flavoured sugar. Let the oil cool before adding the second lot of *bigné*, and repeat the process given above.

They should be served hot sprinkled with sugar.

Enough for 4 people.

Bigné can also be baked and filled with a ricotta or cream filling. Drop the mixture in spoonfuls on to a greased baking sheet, fairly well apart, then bake first for 10 minutes at 400°F. then for a further 20–30 minutes at 350°F. until golden brown. As soon as they come from the oven make a hole in the centre to let the steam out and when cool fill with whipped cream, or sweetened, chocolate-flavoured ricotta, all well beaten.

ZABAIONE

Giuseppe Garibaldi (1807–82), the Italian patriot and hero of the Risorgimento, was in fact born at Nice in France. He entered the Sardinian navy and in 1834 was involved in a disastrous attempt to seize the frigate Euridice with the help of friends aboard, and to occupy the arsenal at Genoa at the same time as Mazzini's army should enter Piedmont. After this he was condemned to death and fled to South America, from where he returned to Italy in 1848. This was only the first of many attempts to unify Italy and to throw off the temporal power of the Pope, who had enlisted the help of France, Austria, Naples and Spain (see also page 74). In 1860, assured by Sir James Hudson of British aid, he reached Marsala, in Sicily on 11th May, under the protection of the British vessels Intrepid and Argus, and his dictatorship was proclaimed the following day. On 15th May the Neapolitan troops were routed at Calatafimi, the first of several victorious battles until he entered Naples on 7th November accompanied by Victor Emmanuel. However, it was not until September 1870 that his troops entered Rome after many vicissitudes and arrests. Thus the unification of Italy began in Marsala with aid from the British.

Marsala wine was created by the English brothers John and William Woodhouse in 1773 and in 1806 Sir Benjamin Ingham founded another cantina. These two companies still exist and several varieties of this delectable wine, which has a delightful taste of burnt sugar (from the small amount of vino cotto added) are good, both to drink and to use in cooking. Woodhouse's 'Garibaldi' is very dark brown with a concentrated taste, but there are also lighter varieties which can be used as an aperitif or as a dessert wine. The famous Italian sweet Zabaione is made with Marsala, and no other wine can give it the essential and original flavour. Garibaldi was immensely popular in England, where a biscuit made with currants was named after him. These, too, can still be found in many shops.

ZABAIONE
(Marsala custard)

2 whole eggs	$\frac{1}{4}$ lb. ($\frac{1}{2}$ cup) (113 g.) caster
4 egg yolks	(extra-fine) sugar
	2 tablespoons Marsala

Zabaione should be made in a porcelain-lined saucepan, and failing this put a bowl inside a saucepan with water up to half-way, or use a double boiler. Put all ingredients into the bowl or double saucepan, cold, then put over a medium flame, and stir all the time, for about 15 minutes until the water boils, by which time the amount will have increased enormously. As soon as it thickens and is light and fluffy pour into warmed glasses and serve. It can also be eaten as above, but frozen.

Serves 4.

See page 102 for further Marsala recipes.

Giuseppe Garibaldi (in cloak) and Menotti with the Mayor of Rome at a banquet given for Garibaldi at the Mausoleum of Augustus, 14th February 1875.

RISOTTO ALLA CERTOSINA

'Here are beautiful sunsets; and here, whichever way you turn your eyes, are scenes as well worth gazing at, both in themselves, and for their historical interest, as any that the sun ever rose and set upon.'
Nathaniel Hawthorne, Notebooks in France and Italy, *1858*

RISOTTO ALLA CERTOSINA
(Rice with prawns)

This is one of the specialities of the Massimo d'Azeglio restaurant, which is renowned for its fish dishes. See also page 93

This risotto can be made with any of the various shrimp or prawn family from the smallest to the largest, but when using the latter cut them in half before cooking.

½ lb. (227 g.) shelled uncooked shrimps or prawns, approx. 12 oz. (340 g.) in the shells
4 tablespoons butter
½ lb. (227 g.) shelled peas
½ lb. (227 g.) skinned tomatoes, or equivalent canned and drained
1½ tablespoons brandy
12 oz. (340 g.) long-grained rice
3 pints (6 cups) (1·6 l.) fish or chicken stock (stock cubes will do) which has been flavoured during cooking with 3 tablespoons white wine
1 bay leaf
1 sprig chopped parsley
3 tablespoons freshly ground Parmesan cheese
salt
freshly ground black pepper

Cook the peas gently with a knob of butter, salt and pepper until they soften. If using fresh tomatoes, skin them by putting them in boiling water for a few minutes, then chop them coarsely (otherwise mash up the drained canned ones), and soften them over a moderate flame for about 5–7 minutes. Bring the stock to the boil with the bay leaf and keep it simmering. Put half the remaining butter in a 5-pint saucepan and when foaming add the rice and stir with a wooden spoon for a few minutes until it is opaque. Then add the stock gradually, stirring well until the rice absorbs it. Cook gently for 15 minutes then add the cheese and cook for a further 5 minutes. Take off the heat and leave uncovered.

Put the rest of the butter in a pan and when foaming add the prawns and cook them lightly for about 5 minutes, stirring well. Add the brandy and let it reduce to half, then add the peas and tomatoes and season to taste. Cover and simmer very gently for about 2 minutes and stir to mix well.

Turn out the rice on to a warmed serving dish and flatten the top, or make a small well in the centre. Pour over the prawns in the sauce, sprinkle with parsley and serve accompanied with more grated Parmesan cheese.

Serves 4.

At the top of the Pincio Gardens with St Peter's Church in the background, c. 1900.

INDEX